FLY FISHING COLORADO'S FRONT RANGE

FLY FISHING COLORADO'S FRONT RANGE

AN ANGLER'S GUIDE

TODD HOSMAN

ILLUSTRATIONS BY ROD WALINCHUS

PRUETT PUBLISHING COMPANY

Boulder, Colorado

Printed in the United States

10 9 8 7 6 5 4 3 2 1

Library of Congress Cataloging-in-Publication data

Hosman, Todd
    Fly fishing Colorado's front range : an angler's guide / by Todd
    Hosman : illustrations by Rod Walinchus.
        Includes bibliographical references.
        ISBN 0-87108-893-2 (pbk.)
        1. Fly fishing—Front Range (Colo. and Wyo.) Guidebooks.
    2. Front Range (Colo. and Wyo.) Guidebooks. I. Title.
    SH464.F76H67   1999
    799.1'1'09788—dc21   99-25299
                                                              CIP

Cover and book design by Studio Signorella
Book composition by Lyn Chaffee
Cover photograph by Stephen Collector
Illustrations by Rod Walinchus

Contents

ACKNOWLEDGMENTS

Thanks to the following businesses and friends for their assistance: Brad Befus, Front Range Anglers, Boulder; Mike Clark, South Creek, Ltd., Lyons; Dale Darling and Mark Raymun, St. Vrain Angler, Longmont; Court Dixon and Mike Chilcoat, Kinsley Outfitters, Boulder; Tom Post, St. Peter's Fly Shop, Fort Collins; and Vance Watson, The Flyfisher, Ltd., Denver.

Dealing with government agencies isn't always easy, but these folks made it a pleasure: Phyllis DeJaynes, Mark Lamb, and Randy Van Buren, Colorado Division of Wildlife; John Bustos, U.S. Forest Service; Ken Czarnowski, National Park Service; and Ken Huson, City of Longmont.

I also thank family, friends, and acquaintances from Colorado and around the country for their valued insights and strong opinions regarding fishing, flies, fly rods, and the outdoors: Dick Alweis, A. K. Best, John Betts, Charles and Ardie Brock, Chris Brown, Rim Chung, Ken Clark, Ed Engle, John Gierach, Jon Harper, George Harvey, Ron Hildebrand, Roger Hill, Dan Hosman, Joe and Ed Jankowski, Charlie Jenkins, Gary LaFontaine, Jack Landblom, Mike Lerdal, John Looney, Eric Neufeld, Mike Price, Jim Pruett, Lee Robinson, John Rough, Rod Walinchus, Joan Wulff, and Vince Zounek.

In preparing this book's information on aquatic insects, I greatly benefited from the wisdom and guidance of a longtime family friend and distinguished scholar, Dr. Edward I. Coher, professor emeritus of biology at Southampton College, New York.

And thanks most of all to Kim Jenkins.

Todd Hosman
Estes Park, Colorado
1998

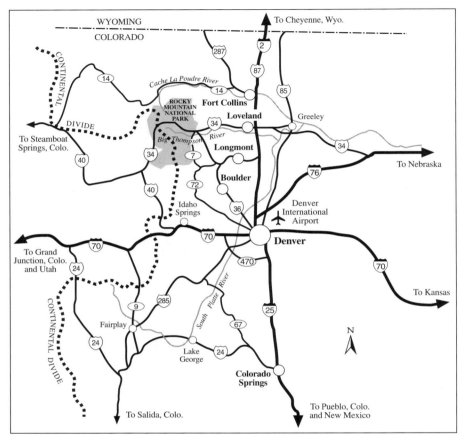

Fig. 1. Colorado's Front Range

Chapter 1

"WHAT A PLACE TO CAST A FLY!"
FLY FISHING COLORADO'S FRONT RANGE

From the range in the west with its
snow-covered summit . . . comes a limpid
stream winding down through the grass-covered
park, its course marked by the deeper green
of the wild grass and the willows. . . .
What a place to cast a fly!
     —L. B. France, *With Rod and Line*
                    in Colorado Waters

FROM COLORADO SPRINGS north to the Wyoming state line, a
chain of foothills and mountains called the Front Range rises to
form the easternmost slopes of the Colorado Rockies. Today
around three million people live in the Front Range metropoli-
tan area, but for about a century nearby wild lands to the west
have been preserved. Hundreds of miles of unspoiled rivers and
streams flow through huge tracts of national forests, wilderness
areas, and other sanctuaries and parks. The waters there offer
ideal habitat for trout—and wonderful opportunities for the fly
angler. Wild and remote as they seem, most Front Range fly-
fishing destinations lie less than a 90-minute drive from the
nearest city.
    A few thousand square miles of land extend from Front
Range cities to the Continental Divide. During your fishing
trips in the region, you'll experience an amazing variety of con-
trasting terrain and conditions. Depending on your destination,
you might fish in waters located anywhere between 5,000 and
11,000 feet above sea level. Aspen and evergreen may grow
along the banks of one stream; cactus and cottonwood along
another. Some waters rush through steep mountain canyons;
others meander through flat, grassy meadows of the high
prairie. Brushy, backwoods creeks barely 5 feet across may hold
fish as large as those found in broad rivers. The trout might

range from 8-inchers to 10-pounders; the most suitable flies range from size #28 midges to size #6 streamers. The prime time to fish could be a sunny summer morning or a snowy mid-winter afternoon.

There's much to know about fly fishing in a place as big and diverse as the Front Range. However, the most successful local fly anglers share the same basic knowledge and skills. They know not only where to fish, but when. They know the region's aquatic insects, the best flies, and the most effective presentation techniques. They also understand how to contend with the challenging environments of the Front Range outdoors. With this book as your guide, you'll develop the same kinds of insights. And you'll enjoy fly fishing here even more.

FLY FISHING THE FRONT RANGE THROUGH THE SEASONS

The nature of Front Range fly fishing varies with the seasons, and understanding the effects of seasonal changes is essential to fly-fishing success. The changes impact critical factors such as trout behavior, water temperature and volume, and insect activity (see Figure 2). Most Front Range rivers and streams (other than tailwaters, which are discussed later in this book) remain icebound from December through February. In a typical year, you can fish free-flowing waters from the months of March through November.

March and April

By early March, ice begins to clear from large sections of rivers and streams at elevations up to around 8,000 feet. (Most ponds and lakes stay frozen until at least June; those at altitudes above 10,000 feet may not become ice-free until July.) From March through April, two of the year's snowiest months, water temperatures usually range from 34 to 39 degrees Fahrenheit. As in winter, trout remain sluggish and occupy deep, slow-moving water. March and April also mark the year's first substantial insect emergences, including those of midges, blue-winged olive mayflies, little brown stoneflies, and a few kinds of small caddisflies. At elevations around 7,000 feet, high daytime air temperatures average 40 degrees in March and 45 degrees in April. By the end of April, nearly all moving waters are free of ice.

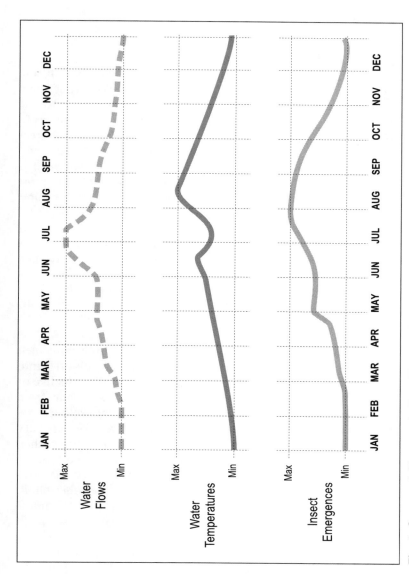

Fig. 2. Seasonal Changes in Free-Flowing Front Range Waters

May

In the first days of May, water temperatures approach 40 degrees, then continue to rise for the next few weeks. Trout begin to leave their deepwater refuges, some keeping close to the stream bottom, others moving into warm shallows near shore. In May, the daily high air temperature regularly exceeds 60 degrees and the chance of snow steadily decreases. As water temperatures reach 50 degrees or more, trout return to what will be their midseason lies in riffles, runs, pools, and glides. (Trout are most likely to feed on or near the surface when water temperatures measure between 47 and 65 degrees.) Hatches occur with greater frequency, and terrestrial insects such as grasshoppers and ants become active. Waters flow at slow to moderate rates; rainbows and cutthroats spawn. As the days grow longer and warmer, plants come into leaf and songbirds return to the Rockies. For a few weeks, dry-fly fishing can be superb. But around the end of the month, it's about time for the start of the big thaw—runoff.

June to Mid-July

During runoff, warm air, strong sunlight, and spring rains melt portions of mountain snowpack, which then "run off" into rivers, ponds, and other drainages. Runoff generally lasts five or six weeks, with the highest flows most often occurring from mid-June to early July. However, depending on the weather and snowpack, a runoff's duration, onset, and intensity can vary greatly from one year to the next and from one place to another. For example, an average winter followed by a cold, snowy spring and a cool summer would probably produce a relatively late-season, long-lasting, and gentle runoff. On the other hand, if the spring was warm and rainy and the summer hot, runoff wouldn't last as long, but it would start sooner and cause much higher and faster stream flows. In any case, you can count on runoff to produce at least several days' worth of extremely high, powerful, and treacherous currents. Don't risk wading in such conditions. Many strong and experienced anglers have been swept off their feet and drowned by the enormous force of runoff waters. Besides, even if you find your favorite stream in the full throes of runoff, there's a chance that perhaps only a few miles away another creek may be flowing more moderately.

Snowmelt not only increases water volumes, it lowers water temperatures, sometimes by as much as 10 degrees. Many trout respond by leaving the main stream and relocating in warmer places such as beaver ponds and temporary pools and creeks formed by overflowing waters. Small and shallow as some of these areas may appear, during runoff they can offer some of the best opportunities for dry-fly fishing. Trout that remain in the stream keep close to the bottom and near streambanks and other shelters. In the high, cold water, weighted nymphs are usually most productive, though dry flies can work well when presented close to shore. By the second week of July, runoff ends and trout disperse to various lies throughout the stream.

Mid-July to October

The year's best dry-fly fishing occurs from mid-July to mid-October, when caddisflies, mayflies, stoneflies, and midges hatch nearly every day. In addition, more than a dozen different terrestrial insects and bugs populate the streambanks. In most streams, water temperatures range from 50 to 60 degrees, and trout feed actively. Days are warm and nights cool. Moderate flows make wading easy. By early autumn, water levels drop noticeably and streamside foliage thins; brown trout and brookies start to spawn. Mayfly emergences begin to dwindle around mid-October, although good hatches of blue-winged olives are still likely. You're bound to find excellent caddis and midge hatches too. Even in late October, dry-fly terrestrial patterns continue to be productive as well.

November to Ice-In

Fly fishing in November takes on much the same aspect that it held in March. Water again runs low and cold. Banks might hold a few inches of snow, and ice forms along some shorelines. Most small ponds and high mountain lakes are ice-covered, or nearly so, and the threat of a snowfall grows greater with each day. In moving waters, dry-fly fishing should focus mainly on midge imitations, though often only a deeply drifted nymph will catch trout. Within the first week or so of December, the fish return to their deepwater retreats to endure another iced-in winter. Then, for a month or two, you and I will tie flies, build rods, read books, and fish the tailwaters. By mid-February, we might wonder why we chose to live so far from the equator; but a week later, we see the ice beginning to break on the wild waters. By the grace of God and the middle of March, another season awaits us.

HEALTH AND SAFETY PRECAUTIONS

In the Rocky Mountains, most outdoor activities—including fly fishing—involve some degree of risk. The hazards faced by anglers might range from minor nuisances to serious, even life-threatening circumstances. The more you know about the potential discomforts and dangers associated with the Front Range outdoors, the better prepared you'll be to deal with them. In many cases, you'll be able to avoid them altogether.

You won't be able to escape the weather, though, and the high desert climate of the Front Range produces extreme weather conditions. Through much of the year, humidity measures below 30 percent and winds periodically gust at more than 60 miles per hour. At elevations 8,000 feet and higher, temperatures often rise and fall more than 40 degrees in the course of a midsummer day. Even in July, light snowfalls aren't rare at elevations above 7,000 feet. To stay safe and comfortable in such an inconstant environment, you'll need to plan carefully and keep a close eye on the weather.

Summer thunderstorms are common along the Front Range, especially during the afternoon. Many produce heavy rain, large hail, high winds, and lightning. At the first sign of a thunderstorm, seek shelter immediately. If you can, move quickly to a lower elevation. A low-lying, brushy area (located away from tall trees or other objects that might attract lightning) makes a good retreat. Stay there until the storm passes. If a storm catches you while you're in an unprotected place, such as a boulder field, crouch low to the ground with your hands on your knees.

Rainstorms can also produce flash floods during or soon after a rainfall, particularly in spring and early summer. In Colorado streams, flash floods are caused by branches and other debris blocking a stream's flow. Upstream waters then gain volume and force sufficient to breach the obstruction, and a powerful surge of water rushes downstream. Although a flash flood is unpredictable, you might notice one of its warnings: a pronounced slackening of stream flow. If you do, move quickly to high ground, especially in canyon areas.

Whatever the weather brings, outfit yourself to stay comfortable and safe. On a fishing trip, always bring a lightweight, hooded jacket that can resist wind and water. Wear breathable fabrics and dress in layers so you can easily remove or add clothing. Keep a pair of fingerless gloves in your jacket or fishing vest. Carry a pair of dry socks with you and keep a complete set of dry clothes in your vehicle or at your campsite. Wear a billed cap or hat and brown-tinted polarized sunglasses. They'll shield your eyes from the area's powerful sunlight and help you see into the water. Even when skies are overcast, use sunscreen. From late spring to early autumn, have some insect repellent handy to keep away ticks and mosquitoes. Wearing subdued colors (such as browns, grays, greens, and blues) helps disguise your presence from the fish. However, when a hunting season is in progress in or near the area you're fishing, wear a blaze-orange vest, cap, or both. Information on the state's hunting seasons is available from the Colorado Division of Wildlife.

Avoid fishing or hiking alone, or if you can't, leave word with a friend regarding your destination and the time you intend to return. Carry a compass and an accurate map of the area where you'll be fishing, particularly when your destination will take you out of sight of your vehicle or the road where it's parked. People often become lost in the forest or canyonlands even though a road, trail, or town may lie just yards away. If you don't know how to read a topographic map or use a compass, learn. Never use a handheld global positioning system (GPS) as your sole navigational device. If the GPS fails, you'll still need a compass and map for backup. Other survival tools that fit easily into a fishing vest include waterproof matches, a space blanket, a Swiss army knife, a 10-foot length of rope, a flashlight with spare bulb and batteries, a first-aid kit, and a loud whistle. You should also carry some food and drinking water. Keep in mind that cellular telephones function best in flat, open terrain. In the canyons that surround most Front Range fishing destinations, cell phones work poorly or not at all.

Water and Altitude

Clear and clean as most Front Range waters appear, many contain *Giardia*, a microorganism from the excrement of beavers and other mammals that causes severe intestinal disorders in humans. Drinking untreated water can cause giardiasis—nausea, vomiting, fever, and diarrhea. Always pretreat stream water you plan to use for drinking or cooking. Many good, portable water filters can remove virtually all contaminants, including *Giardia*, from stream water. Small, light, and relatively inexpensive, most of these devices can filter at least a quart of water per minute. Iodine tablets are another easy way to purify water. Both are available at most sporting goods stores.

Most of the fishing destinations described in this book lie at altitudes between 5,000 and 11,000 feet. In these oxygen-poor environments, take time to rest and recover when you begin to tire. The high altitude, low humidity, frequent winds, and strong sunlight of the Rockies can quickly dehydrate your body. Allowing yourself to become even slightly dehydrated is physically harmful, especially at high altitudes. During the course of a day's fishing, drink at least one or two quarts of water, even if you don't feel thirsty. Staying hydrated can also help ward off altitude sickness, a potentially serious illness that can affect anyone, anytime. Its symptoms include nausea, irregular heartbeat, dizziness, weakness, headache, shortness of breath, and fatigue. If you think you have altitude sickness while you're fishing or hiking, get to a lower elevation quickly and drink plenty of water. If the symptoms persist, consult a physician. Altitude sickness generally subsides after a few days' acclimation to elevations above 5,000 feet.

While in the outdoors, beware of hypothermia, which can occur at any time of year, even when air temperatures are above 50 degrees. Hypothermia results from a dangerous lowering of body temperature. To avoid becoming hypothermic, protect yourself from winds, dress warmly and comfortably, eat and drink well, and stay dry. Never wear wet clothing; moisture hastens the loss of body heat. If you feel chilled, overtired, or uncomfortable, you may be experiencing the early stages of hypothermia. Take a break or head home. Severe hypothermia can be serious, even fatal.

Wildlife

In Colorado, feeding wildlife or approaching it too closely is illegal. The acts are not only dangerous to humans but extremely harmful to the animals as well. During your fishing trips along the Front Range, you'll see a huge variety of wildlife, including deer and elk. Moose are less common but are also present, particularly in areas that are heavily wooded and wet. Two other large regional mammals, black bears and pumas (mountain lions), are shy and seen only occasionally. I've never had an uncomfortably close encounter with either, nor have any of my friends, many of whom have fished the

Front Range backcountry for more than forty years. In all of Colorado, wild animal attacks on humans are extremely rare and, when they occur, there's usually a source for provocation. In the state's recorded history, pumas have killed two people. (One was jogging, the other running. Both actions may trigger a puma's instinct to attack.) In twentieth-century Colorado, two people have been killed by bears. Nearly every instance of a marauding or "problem" bear can be attributed to improperly secured food or garbage. A female bear also may behave aggressively when she senses a threat to her cubs.

When you walk through wild areas—especially where visibility is limited by heavy vegetation or bends in the trail—alert animals to your presence. Talk, sing, or make noise. If they know you're around, most animals will avoid you. If you see a bear, back off calmly, slowly, and quietly. (A bear that stands upright or moves closer to you may only be trying to determine what you are.) Don't make direct eye contact. As you move away, speak in a soft, reassuring voice. Never turn your back, run, or climb a tree. Use the same tactics if you see a puma, and try to make yourself look larger by raising your arms or by holding your shirt or jacket open. If a puma begins to act aggressively toward you, throw things at it; just don't crouch or kneel to pick them up.

But what to do if you are attacked by a bear, puma, or other wild creature? The Colorado Division of Wildlife offers clear advice: Fight back. According to the Division, the weapons successfully used by people to defend themselves from an animal include sticks, stones, hats, binoculars, knives, coats, and bare hands.

Rattlesnakes inhabit some areas of the Front Range at elevations between 5,000 and 7,000 feet. They too are shy creatures, more interested in mice than in us. In rattler country, take special care to watch where you step and place your hands. In 1996 less than a dozen people in the country died from venomous snakebites; far more were killed by lightning. According to the American Red Cross and most physicians, the typical snakebite first-aid kit has little or no value. On the remote chance a rattler bites you, get medical attention as soon as you can.

RODS, REELS, LINES, AND OTHER GEAR

In large part, choosing the right tackle is a matter of personal preference. Some of my friends wouldn't dream of casting anything other than cane; others insist that only the latest graphite rods will do. Similarly strong opinions carry over to selecting reels, lines, and leaders. Whatever your tastes, the equipment you use should be adapted to the fishing challenge at hand. An 8-foot rod rated for a 5-weight line is well suited to most Front Range trout fishing. However, the ideal choice of fly rod changes according to where, when, and how you fish. A 5- or 6-foot rod can prove invaluable for small, brushy creeks. In places with more room to cast, a fly rod that measures from 7 to 9 feet long might work most efficiently. Generally, you should reserve the use of 2- or 3-weight rods for calm or slow-moving waters, times of little or no wind, and catching trout smaller than 16 inches. Many experienced Front Range anglers favor a 4-weight rod for its ability to present flies delicately, play large trout effectively, and withstand casting in moderately windy conditions. A 6-weight rod, the heaviest that you'll ever need for Front Range trout, has the power to cast against strong winds and to throw large, weighted flies. Whatever rod you select should be rated for the lightest line-weight practical in your particular fishing situation. Some multipiece rods perform as well as two-piece models and can be more convenient for traveling.

Use a high-quality, single-action reel backed with 20-pound-test braided Dacron. The reel should feature a reliable and smooth drag system. A sinking-tip line (with a sink rate of around 4 inches per second) comes in handy for fishing ponds and lakes, especially early in the season, as well as for streamer fishing in creeks and rivers. However, a floating fly line can accommodate most Front Range fly fishing. When selecting a line, remember that weight-forward lines are designed mainly for distance, not for delicacy or responsiveness. Sometimes casts of 50 feet or longer will be helpful, but in most cases, you'll seldom need to cast farther than 30 feet. Double-taper or triangle-taper lines mend and roll-cast better than weight-forward lines; they can also help you execute the most delicate presentations. Whatever their design, a large number of fly lines become stiff, coiled, and unmanageable at temperatures below 50 degrees. Relatively soft lines (such as the Cortland 444 and Wulff brands) don't have this problem. Many fly-line manufacturers claim their products require little or no maintenance. However, after repeated exposure to the waters of rivers, streams, and ponds, a line's surface accumulates dried algae and other debris. The line not only loses buoyancy but also becomes increasingly difficult to cast, shoot, and control. The forward 20 or 30 feet of a fly line receive the most use and collect the most dirt. Periodic cleaning and application of line dressing greatly improve a fly line's performance.

Depending on the circumstances, the most appropriate leaders for Front Range fly fishing could measure from 4 to 14 feet long. Commonly used tippet sizes vary from 3X (for heavy, deepwater nymphs) to 7X (for tiny dry flies or emergers). For all-round use, select an 8- to 9-foot monofilament leader tapered to 4X or 5X. Compared to a knotless leader, a knotted leader is easier to repair or rebuild in the field. Knotted leaders also offer better visibility on the water and comparable casting ease. A knotless leader is best adapted to slipping through weed-laden waters without becoming fouled. A George Harvey–style leader, which consists of knotted sections of monofilament (stiff mono for the butt section, and limp for the tip), remains a favorite of many local anglers, particularly for dry-fly fishing.

The relatively shallow depth of many waters allows for the use of hip waders, but chest-high waders are more versatile. Through most of the year, you can use waders made of Gore-Tex or similar fabric. They weigh a fraction of neoprene models but don't promote perspiration. They also pack down to a size small enough to fit in your day pack or the back of your vest—a helpful feature when your destination lies a 1- or 2-mile hike away. For winter fishing, when you might stand in icy water for an hour or more at a time, 3 mm neoprene waders are still the best choice. Because many rivers and creeks have slippery, rock-lined streambeds, wading boots with studded felt soles are useful. However, the best such boots are heavy (especially when wet) and impractical to wear or carry during a hike that lasts more than an hour or so. Some companies manufacture lightweight, collapsible, felt-soled wading boots. These stow easily in a pack or vest and work well during backcountry fishing trips.

Many of the fishing destinations described in this book require hiking, and a good quality pack and comfortable walking shoes or boots can make your trip more enjoyable. When selecting a pack, look for features such as large, heavy-duty zippers; big, easily opened compartments; adjustable cinch straps (to help balance the pack's load); and well-padded carrying straps. A 2,000-cubic-inch backpack is about the right size for a day trip. It can hold wading boots, fabric waders, rod tube, fishing vest, lunch, water purifier, reel, spools, maps, jacket, and a few pieces of dry clothing. Bring some plastic bags for storing wet boots and waders. When loaded with this kind of gear, your pack will probably weigh about 12 to 14 pounds. A stout hiking stick gives you added stability on the trail and can double as a wading staff.

Chapter II
FRONT RANGE TROUT AND TROUT FISHING

Of course, every once in a while a fly fisherman catches
a trout on a trout fly, and he thinks this proves something.
—Ed Zern, *To Hell with Fishing*

IN THE MIDDLE 1800s, the only trout found in Colorado were four kinds of cutthroats: greenback, Colorado River, Rio Grande, and the now-extinct yellowfin. The most common Front Range trout species today are not native to the area but were brought here by sportsmen of the late nineteenth and early twentieth centuries. Through the years, many of these introduced (or "exotic") fish have become wild and self-sustaining. They include browns from Germany, rainbows from California, and brookies from the eastern United States. About a century ago, this introduction of exotic fish, combined with habitat destruction and overfishing, nearly eradicated the Front Range's indigenous trout, the greenback cutthroat. Though making a strong comeback, today the greenback remains a threatened species. If you catch one, the law demands that you immediately return it unharmed to the water. You can identify a cutthroat trout by the bright crimson color that spreads across the fish's gills and beneath its jaw. However, for the layperson, distinguishing between various kinds of cutthroat trout is often impossible. A rainbow trout can resemble a cutthroat; so can a cuttbow, a hybrid of the two fish. For these reasons, if you land a trout that you think might be a greenback, release it.

Whatever the species, a trout's appearance varies according to its gender, diet, habitat, and age. Spawning brings about changes in a trout's coloration and shape as well. Altogether, these factors can make a difficult matter of identifying trout. However, browns, rainbows, and brookies exhibit some unique physical characteristics. For example, a brook trout has lower-body fins tipped with black and white. A brown trout's body is bronze-colored and sparsely dotted with red and black. A dif-fuse pink stripe marks the sides of a rainbow trout from near its tail to its gills. Other fish you may encounter during your Front Range trout-fishing trips include Rocky Mountain white-fish, pike, grayling, splake (a cross between a lake trout and a brookie), and kokanee salmon.

WHIRLING DISEASE

For as much as we might cherish fly fishing—its solitude, beauty, and tradition—fishing is big business. In 1991, for ex-ample, Colorado recreational anglers contributed nearly three-quarters of a billion dollars to the state and the national economies. Like many other western states, Colorado relies on outdoor sports such as fishing to bolster an even more lucra-tive industry: tourism. And what better way to assure angler success and tourist revenue than by stocking thousands of "catchable-size," hatchery-bred rainbow trout in lakes, rivers, and streams? You may already know why so many fly anglers and naturalists object to hatchery fish. Wild trout are stronger and smarter, and a natural part of a healthy ecosystem. In con-trast, hatchery trout are unnatural and intrusive. They disrupt wild trout populations and habitat; they're also comparatively stupid and easy to catch. However, with hundreds of millions of dollars at stake—and thousands of "sport fishermen" ex-pecting to kill their limit on every trip—many western trout-stocking programs have persisted. But as so often happens when man interferes with nature, a serious and potentially grave problem developed: whirling disease. In 1975, Ohio was the westernmost state that had confirmed the disease's pres-ence in its hatchery trout. Twelve years later Colorado faced the same trouble. By 1998, twenty-two states across America had reported the presence of whirling disease in their hatch-eries and rivers.

Whirling disease (WD) may occur naturally, but in the United States virtually every instance of it can be traced to WD-contaminated hatchery trout. Restricted to European hatcheries until the 1950s, WD is caused by a metazoan parasite. Spores from the parasite are eaten by tubifex worms, threadlike aquatic worms that live on the bottoms of streams and lakes. Ingestion of the worm (or exposure to its parasitic spores) in-fects trout. The fish then become carriers of the parasite as well.

In addition, WD can be spread by predatory or scavenging birds and mammals, who after eating diseased fish, may discharge parasite-laden excrement in other waters. Once within a trout, the parasite eats away at the fish's cartilage, especially in the head and tail areas of young trout. Deformity, discoloration, and death often result. During the disease's course, an infected fish may lose its equilibrium and begin to chase its tail, whirling in circles when it tries to swim. Some fish that survive WD become weakened and more vulnerable to predators or environmental stress. In several western rivers, WD has decimated wild rainbow populations.

Generally, it appears that rainbow trout are most susceptible to WD, though the disease can also infect cutthroats. Other trout, including browns and brookies, are not immune but may be more resistant to WD. Today WD is present in countless western waters. But the mere presence of WD parasites in a water or a trout does not necessarily mean that either is doomed. Some trout (rainbows in California, for example) apparently tolerate the parasites better than others. It's speculated that the larger and more varied a trout's gene pool is, the better is its tolerance to WD. A few years ago, Colorado fishery managers received widespread negative press for their decision to stock WD-positive trout in selected streams. At first glance, the idea seemed senseless. Critics said the fishery managers had yielded to political and business interests. But some biologists argued (and correctly, perhaps) that those fish had demonstrated a genetic resistance to the WD parasite and that stocking them could benefit trout populations.

At this writing, research to combat WD is progressing gradually. In hatcheries, ultraviolet light has been used with some success to kill WD spores. Researchers are also looking into drug treatments and DNA testing. However, no one yet seems sure what to do about rivers and streams already threatened by the disease. Biologists surmise that the parasitic spore (*Myxobolus cerebralis*) can survive in or out of water, in conditions of extreme heat or cold, for thirty years or more. Nevertheless, scientists at the Whirling Disease Foundation, in Bozeman, Montana, are optimistic. Among their goals are the identification of genetically resistant trout species, the interruption of the parasite's life cycle, and the analysis of environmental factors that promote the disease.

To help reduce the spread of WD, anglers should clean potentially contaminated mud and debris from their boots, waders, boats, and other equipment before moving from one water to another. Of course, catch-and-release fishing can help diminish—or even preclude—the need for hatchery-bred trout. (Incidentally, handling or eating trout infected with WD poses no threat to humans.) You can also fight WD by making tax-deductible contributions to the Whirling Disease Foundation, P.O. Box 327, Bozeman, Montana 59771.

FISHING REGULATIONS

Before you head streamside, you'll need to have a license as well as a basic knowledge of state fishing regulations. In Colorado, anglers sixteen years of age and older must carry a Colorado fishing license. A one-year license remains valid for the calendar year in which it was purchased. One-day and five-day fishing licenses also are available. Annual fishing license fees are set through the year 2000 at:

Colorado resident	$20.25
Colorado resident, age 64 or older	$10.25
Nonresident	$40.25

You can buy licenses at most sporting goods stores. With your license, pick up the most recent copy of the *Colorado Fishing Season Information & Wildlife Property Directory*. Distributed by the Colorado Division of Wildlife, the free brochure contains an alphabetized listing of many Colorado waters and notes on special restrictions. It also details Colorado fishing regulations. Where special regulations are not in effect, these fundamental rules apply to Front Range trout fishing through the year 2000:

Season	Year-round
Bag limit	Up to 8 fish, any size
Possession limit	Up to 8 fish, any size

The bag limit refers to the quantity of trout an angler may catch and keep during the course of a day. The possession limit is the total number of trout an angler may retain at any time. Bag and possession limits are interdependent. For example, an angler who has seven trout at home in the freezer would be allowed to catch and keep only one additional trout during his or her next fishing trip. Although the Colorado fishing season lasts year-round, some waters remain closed to fishing during part or all of the year. It's always the angler's responsibility to know and follow regulations that govern waters where he or she may choose to fish. Special regulations usually mandate the use of flies or lures exclusively, limitations on the size or number of trout that can be kept, or catch-and-release fishing. Never trespass on private property. Get permission before fishing in private waters.

CATCH-AND-RELEASE FISHING

Wherever you fish along the Front Range and whatever the regulations stipulate, always practice catch-and-release fishing. As Lee Wulff observed in 1938, "A good gamefish is too valuable to be caught only once." Habitually keeping and killing trout not only robs other anglers of potential fishing opportunities, it also perpetuates the stocking of hatchery fish, which can harm wild trout populations. Catch-and-release fishing helps promote the proliferation of wild trout, and wild trout are the soul of fly fishing. Fishing for hatchery trout is about as sporting as hunting on an elk farm.

Proper catch-and-release technique involves more than just tossing a fish back into the water. Always use the stoutest tippet practical to a fishing situation and land the trout as quickly as you can. Playing a trout too long may exhaust and eventually kill it. Leave the fish in the water during all or most of the release process. If you must remove a trout from the water, wet your hands before touching it. Handle the fish gently but firmly, cradling the upper part of its body in your palm and making sure to keep your fingers out of its gills. Holding the fish upside-down may help calm it. Take a moment to observe how the hook entered, then carefully back it out the way it went in. If a trout is so deeply hooked as to make the hook's removal impossible without harming the fish, cut the tippet close to the hook and leave the hook in place. With the fish rightside-up and fully submerged, gently support the fish as it recovers. Allow about as much time for its revival as you took to land it. Slowly moving a fish back and forth in the water can help reoxygenate it. After the fish makes one or two strong attempts to swim away, release it.

Using de-barbed hooks makes catch-and-release fishing easier. You can remove a hook barb by crimping it with a pair of pliers or forceps. You might also tie or purchase barbless-hook flies. Compared to a barbed hook, a de-barbed or barbless hook has superior penetration qualities and can be removed from a fish (or yourself) more easily.

ANGLING ETIQUETTE

Unlike many sports, fly fishing has no strict rules of personal conduct, no referees or umpires to judge or enforce our streamside behavior. However, you can't go far wrong if you follow a basic guideline: On the stream, show other anglers the same courtesy and consideration you'd expect from them. When possible, stay at least a couple hundred yards away from and out of the sight of other people fishing. If you have the chance to speak with them, ask how far and in which direction they intend to fish. Then adjust your plans to accommodate theirs. While fishing a productive piece of water, especially one in a popular place, realize that other anglers may be awaiting their turn to fish it as well. Don't stay there too long. Never wade or cast in or near an area that's occupied by an angler without first gaining his or her approval. If while hiking along a shoreline you see a person fishing a section of water, keep far from the banks. Never allow the sight of your shadow or the sound of your footsteps to disturb the trout in someone's chosen spot. If a fishing site is so crowded as to prevent you from extending these kinds of courtesies, leave.

Chapter III
FOODS AND FLIES FOR FRONT RANGE TROUT

*Wisdom is the principal thing; therefore get wisdom; and with
all thy getting get understanding.*
                    —Proverbs 4:7

FRONT RANGE RIVERS and streams teem with various aquatic insects, many unique to the Rocky Mountain region. A basic understanding of the insects and their imitations can make your
Front Range angling experiences more rewarding. Whatever
time of year you happen to be fishing, take time to investigate
and examine the foods available to trout. In the field, you won't
always be able to identify the insects you discover, especially
those in pre-adult life stages. But close observation of an insect's
size, shape, and color can help you select the most suitable imitation. Similarly, an insect's behavior exemplifies the elements
of a lifelike and appealing presentation.

Let's say it's a sunny midafternoon in early July, and
you're fishing a fast stream at an elevation of about 9,000 feet.
You notice large (size #12 or so) yellowish mayflies flying above
the water. Trout aren't yet rising, but being hopeful and a good
sport, you tie on a dry fly that matches the natural insect. However, your well-placed, perfectly drifted presentations arouse no
interest, not even a refusal. Neither do the naturals. What's
happening here? Chances are the mayflies are newly emerged
quill gordons (*Epeorus* sp.). Though trout often rise to the
duns, sometimes they focus instead on eating the insects' preemergent nymphs, which gather near slack waters and near the
shore. If you had drifted an appropriate nymph through these
areas, you probably would have done better. Consistent fly-
fishing success relies more on logic than on luck.

Sometimes, though, merely locating the insects (or other
foods) that trout may be eating can be tricky. In these instances,
search rocks, branches, vegetation, and other potential insect

habitat found on or near the streambed. Look in spider webs too. To capture subsurface insect specimens, use a wire-handled aquarium dip-net, holding the net underwater for at least a few minutes before you retrieve and inspect its contents. You can also use the net to catch insects as they float, fly, or move about on the shore. Sold at pet shops, a dip-net weighs only a couple of ounces and costs two or three dollars. In addition, unless you're extremely nearsighted, you'll probably need some sort of small magnifier for viewing insects that measure less than 8 millimeters (about 5/16 inch) long. That's where a collapsible printer's loupe comes in handy. It takes up only about as much space as a pocket watch but provides 4X magnification, which is adequate for most streamside uses.

The next five sections describe aquatic and terrestrial insects and other foods commonly available to Front Range trout. They also detail emergence periods, fishing techniques, and the most effective regional fly patterns. To convey information accurately, scientific names accompany the common names of aquatic insects. For instance, in Colorado the common name "red quill mayfly" might refer to a size #12 species that hatches from July to August, or to another mayfly that's half as large and emerges a month or so earlier. Using an insect's scientific name helps prevent this kind of confusion. As typified by the form "Family: *Genus species*," a scientific name parses out the characteristics of an insect from the general to the specific. "Ephemerellidae: *Ephemerella inermis*" (a pale morning dun) refers to the insect family Ephemerellidae (which has about ten members in Front Range waters), the genus *Ephemerella* (of which there are three regional species), and the species *inermis* (which is the actual insect in question). The abbreviation "sp." indicates that two or more species of an insect exist and that the differences between them hold little importance to Front Range fly fishing. For instance, "*Sweltsa* sp." refers to several species of stoneflies commonly known as the yellow sally.

Although based upon years of firsthand observation by experienced Front Range fly anglers, the emergence periods listed here can serve only as guidelines. Front Range waters flow in wild, unpredictable environments shaped by climatic extremes. Don't be surprised if a particular hatch comes off weeks earlier or later than the times indicated in this book's emergence charts. Descriptions of an insect's coloration represent generalized information. An insect's color often varies in intensity and hue from one water to another, and even with an adult insect, from one stage of maturity to the next. An insect's length is cited both in millimeters (mm) and corresponding hook size. According to their environments and the foods available to them, aquatic insects of the same species may differ from their specified sizes by 10 percent or more. Unless noted otherwise, the Mustad style 94840 dry-fly hook serves as the model hook for an insect's imitation. Some of the fly patterns mentioned here are peculiar to the Front Range and Rocky Mountain regions; others have somehow lost popularity among most American fly anglers. Fly-tying recipes accompany only those patterns that are generally viewed as regional or uncommon.

FRONT RANGE CADDISFLIES

Judging by the popular acclamation of savvy local anglers and discerning trout, in Colorado caddisflies reign supreme. Caddisflies adapt to varied environments, but they flourish in the cool, rocky-bottomed waters of most Front Range rivers and streams. In fact, more than seventy-five species live there, though only ten or so main varieties of the insect are of special interest to the angler. If you have trouble distinguishing between the adult forms of a caddisfly and stonefly, study the wing position of the insect while it's not in flight. A caddisfly's wings are often referred to as "tent-like": they're angled off to the sides of its body in the shape of an inverted V. In contrast, a typical stonefly holds its wings flat, positioned above and perpendicular to its body. Caddisfly emergences usually begin in late March or early April and continue well into October. The most common sizes of adult caddisflies (as measured from the tip of the insect's head to the end of its wings) are from 8 to 16 mm long (hook sizes #18 to #10), with the insect's antennae generally at least half as long as its wings. The insect's wings may be of a single color (most commonly, tan, gray, or brown), but they may also be spotted or mottled with a combination of these colors. When anglers see a caddisfly, they commonly and mistakenly correlate the color of the insect's wing with that of the insect's body (which they fail to examine). However, the dominant color of an adult caddis body is usually a shade of

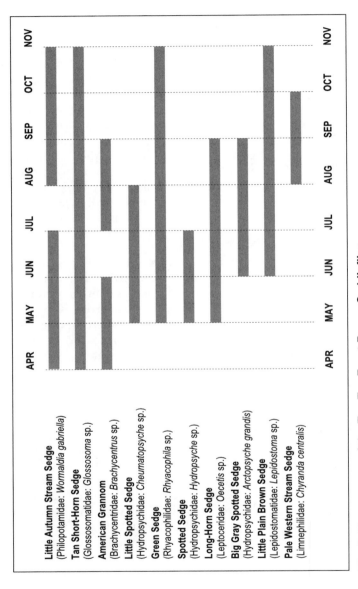

Fig. 3. Emergences of the Top Ten Front Range Caddisflies

| Caddisflies: | Larva | | | Pupa | | | | Adult | | | | | Size | Adult Color | Egg-Laying | Category |
	Herl Nymph	Caddis Larva, Dark Olive	Caddis Larva, Green	Rubber Band Nymph	Partridge-and-Orange	ESP, Brown and Green	ESP, Brown and Yellow	Wet Cahill Variant	Deer-Hair Caddis	Colorado King	Henryville Special	Spent Partridge Caddis				
Little Autumn Stream Sedge (Philopotamidae: *Wormaldia gabriella*)	■			■	■	■		■	■		■	■	#18 to #16 (8 to 10mm)	Light to dark olive body; mottled gray-brown wings	Subsurface	Net-spinning
Tan Short-Horn Sedge (Glossosomatidae: *Glossosoma sp.*)				■	■	■		■	■		■	■	#18 to #14 (8 to 12mm)	Light to dark tan body; tan wings	Subsurface	Saddle-case
American Grannom (Brachycentridae: *Brachycentrus sp.*)			■		■	■	■	■	■	■	■		#16 to #12 (10 to 14mm)	Brilliant green to olive body; tan to olive wings	Surface	Tube-case
Little Spotted Sedge (Hydropsychidae: *Cheumatopsyche sp.*)					■	■		■	■		■		#18 to #16 (8 to 10mm)	Green to olive body; brown wings	Subsurface	Net-spinning
Green Sedge (Rhyacophilidae: *Rhyacophila sp.*)		■	■		■				■	■			#18 to #10 (8 to 16mm)	Tan to olive body; mottled gray-brown wings	Subsurface	Free-living
Spotted Sedge (Hydropsychidae: *Hydropsyche sp.*)					■	■			■	■			#16 to #12 (10 to 14mm)	Gray-brown to yellow-brown body; mottled brown wings	Subsurface	Net-spinning
Long-Horn Sedge (Leptoceridae: *Oecetis sp.*)	■				■	■			■	■			#16 to #14 (9 to 12mm)	Brown to yellow body and wings	Surface	Tube-case
Big Gray Spotted Sedge (Hydropsychidae: *Arctopsyche grandis*)		■			■	■		■	■		■		#12 to #10 (15 to 20mm)	Light to medium olive body; gray, spotted wings	Subsurface	Net-spinning
Little Plain Brown Sedge (Lepidostomatidae: *Lepidostoma sp.*)	■				■	■				■	■		#18 to #16 (8 to 9mm)	Light brown to yellow-tan body and wings	Surface or onshore	Tube-case
Pale Western Stream Sedge (Limnephilidae: *Chyranda centralis*)	■				■		■			■			#12 to #10 (15 to 20mm)	Pale yellow body; mottled tan wings	Onshore	Tube-case

Fig. 4. The Top Ten Front Range Caddisflies and Their Primary Imitations

green, brown, or yellow, any of which may vary greatly in intensity. After developing from an egg, a caddisfly remains a larva for the better part of a year. The larva becomes a pupa for a month or so and then emerges into an adult. Compared to the length of the adult insect, a caddis larva is frequently one or two hook sizes larger; a caddis pupa, often about one hook size smaller. For summary information regarding prominent regional caddisflies, refer to Figures 3 and 4. After that crash course in caddisflies, you just might want to grab some tackle and go fishing. On the other hand, a more in-depth knowledge of caddisfly life stages and their imitations assures you of far greater success and enjoyment on the stream. In Colorado, the angler who comprehends the caddis catches the most trout.

Clues of the Caddis Case

The typical caddis larva lives beneath the water in a sheltering case that the insect builds around its body with vegetation, sand, silk, pebbles, or some combination of these materials. As the larva grows, it enlarges its case. Look for the cases (and the creatures within them)

Tube-Case Caddis

Tube-Case Caddis

on and under rocks, branches, plants, or debris in streambeds. Caddis cases can give you a good indication of the types of caddisflies that reside in a particular water. The caddis cases of most importance to the Front Range fly angler are those built by three groups of caddisflies: tube-case caddis, net-spinning caddis, and saddle-case caddis.

Net-Spinning Caddis

Probably the most recognizable caddis case is the finely crafted, tapered, and chimney-shaped shelter built by the American grannom. Three other Front Range tube-case caddisflies include the long-horn sedge, little plain brown sedge, and pale western stream sedge.

Saddle-Case Caddis

Compared to a grannom's tidy, symmetrical shelter, some of their cases may appear roughly formed, though their interiors are indeed tubular and neat.

A net-spinning caddisfly weaves a small, food-catching net or web near an opening in its case. (If the case is removed from the water, the web seldom remains intact.) The shelter built by the typical net-spinner looks like a little stack of pebbles that might have been randomly thrown together by the currents. Consequently, the cases are overlooked by anglers. Nevertheless, net-spinning caddisflies contribute to some of the best fly-fishing opportunities along the Front Range. These insects include the little autumn stream sedge, little spotted sedge, spotted sedge, and big gray spotted sedge.

The most prominent Front Range saddle-case caddis is the tan short-horn sedge. Its pebbly shelter is fairly symmetrical and often likened to the form of a helmet, tortoise shell, or barnacle.

Unlike other caddisflies, the green sedge spends all its larval life as a roaming, free-living predator without any kind of protective case. After about ten months, a green sedge larva develops into a pupa and builds a case similar to the shelter of a net-spinning caddis. The pupa remains encased for about four weeks prior to emergence.

Caddisfly Life Stages and Their Imitations

The Cased Caddis—Trout often eat caddis cases whole—one good reason why a cased-caddis pattern can be so effective. For example, tube-case caddis larvae periodically release themselves, cases and all, into the flows, apparently in search of more food and a better neighborhood. The trout await them.

Pattern: Herl Nymph

Presentations: Up-and-across presentations generally work best. Get into the habit of presenting a Herl Nymph delicately and carefully, almost as though it were a dry fly. Cased-caddis imitations can be used to great effect in low-water or still-water conditions.

Herl Nymph Recipe

Hook: Dry-fly hook, sizes #16 to #10.
Thread: Black.
Body: Peacock herl ribbed with gold or copper wire.
Beard: Partridge fibers.
Collar: Brown or black ostrich herl.

Comments:
The fly's body can be trimmed to shape with a razor or fine scissors. If you need a Herl Nymph but don't have one, remove the tails (and the wings, if you like) from a Prince Nymph.

The Caddis Larva — Free-living, uncased larvae of the green sedge often lose their grip on the streambed; other caddis larvae frequently leave or become dislodged from their cases. The insects then drift helplessly wherever the currents take them, many falling prey to vigilant trout. Not surprisingly, caddis larva patterns rate among the region's most productive subsurface flies.

Patterns: Caddis Larva, Rubber Band Nymph

Presentations:
In imitation of the natural insect, a caddis larva pattern is best presented in a dead drift, either up- or down-and-across the currents. Trout will also take the fly during its retrieve, which should be executed slowly, at the rate of just an inch or so every few seconds.

Rubber Band Nymph Recipe
Hook: Caddis-larva hook or wet-fly hook, sizes #16 to #8.
Thread: Black.
Body: A narrow length of rubber band wound along most
          of the hook shank.
Ribbing: Gold or copper wire.
Beard: Partridge fibers.
Collar: Peacock herl.

Comments:
A Latex Caddis Larva (which is tied similarly, but with a strip
of tan sheet-latex wound over a green-floss underbody) can perform as well as a Rubber Band Nymph. However, after just several weeks, the rubbery bodies of both patterns deteriorate. In
imitation of the drifting insect's curled body, caddis-larva patterns are often tied on curved hooks.

The Emerging Caddis Pupa—After nine or ten months, a caddis larva transforms into a pupa, and like a pre-emergent but-
terfly in a cocoon, remains dormant in a well-secured case.
Within a month or so, the fully mature pupa opens the case and
then drifts and swims toward the water's surface. (Comparatively few caddisflies emerge on shore.) During a caddis hatch,
trout typically ignore any adult caddisflies and instead focus
upon eating the defenseless emergers.

Patterns: Partridge-and-Orange, LaFontaine's Emergent
          Sparkle Pupa

Presentations:
Caddisfly emergences can be complex and sometimes confounding, affected by the habits of the particular caddis species, water and weather conditions, and countless other variables. Understanding some basic emergence characteristics can help you optimize your caddis-emerger presentations. For example, typical caddis emergence is distinguished by a period of drifting followed by an ascension to or near the surface. These movements can be simulated by a down-and-across presentation. However, an emerger may drift at relatively deep levels in the water for varying lengths of time. Then an up-and-across, dead-drift presentation can be productive. As you seek the ideal presentation depth, don't hesitate to increase, reduce, or reposition the weight clinched onto your tippet. Sometimes caddis emergers drift for several minutes just below the water's surface (or "film") or on the surface itself. During these occasions, use up-and-across techniques, presenting the emerger pattern as though it were a dry fly. A microshot clinched onto the tippet about a foot above the fly can help to keep the fly in the film. If conditions warrant it, present the fly unweighted, perhaps dressed with a bit of floatant.

Pattern Notes:
The Partridge-and-Orange can also be persuasive when tied with a green or yellow body. Most of the time, however, regardless of the colors present in the natural caddis emergers, a Partridge-and-Orange gets the job done. It's a great fly. Tie them, buy them, use them. When chosen in an appropriate size and thoughtfully presented, the Partridge-and-Orange can help you solve not only the emergence mysteries of caddisflies but also those of mayflies and even midges.

Gary LaFontaine's Emergent Sparkle Pupa (ESP) is another outstanding pattern. The dominant colors of the fly's body are usually shades of green or yellow. The deer-hair wing and marabou collar are brown. The Green-and-Brown ESP (green body, brown wing and collar) is the best all-round choice for imitating Front Range caddis emergers, though a yellow-and-brown version (yellow body, brown wing and collar) can also work well, depending upon the colors of the emerging caddisflies.

The Subsurface Adult Caddis—Comparatively few kinds of caddisflies remain on the water's surface to lay eggs. Instead, most

Front Range caddisflies dive, swim, or crawl to the streambed. After depositing eggs there, they return to the surface or shore. This kind of egg-laying process gives trout many options for feeding. They might prefer to eat the caddisflies that have reached the stream bottom, or the caddis moving down toward it, or the caddis rising away from it. The trout could also be attracted to the caddisflies that have returned to the water's surface. To make matters even more intriguing, periods of caddisfly egg laying sometimes coincide with caddisfly emergences. For the moment, though, let's deal with the subsurface adult caddis.

Pattern: Wet Cahill Variant

Presentations:
The Wet Cahill Variant is best fished weighted in a relatively short-line, up-and-across presentation. As the fly drifts, slowly lift the rod tip high, then slowly lower it (so that the fly will alternately rise and sink). As the fly nears the completion of its drift, raise the rod tip again. A down-and-across presentation of a lightly weighted or unweighted fly is well adapted to fishing shallow waters.

Wet Cahill Variant Recipe
Hook: Dry-fly or wet-fly hook, sizes #18 to #10.
Thread: Black.
Body: Olive brown dubbing ribbed with gold or copper wire.
Underwing: Orange Antron.
Overwing: Mallard flank.
Beard: Brown hackle fibers.

Comments:
This fly is a variation on the traditional Wet Cahill.

The Surface Adult Caddis—Caddisflies mate near the water, but not in or on it. Large numbers of adult caddisflies are found on the water's surface in just a couple of situations: during periods of emergence or when laying eggs. Regardless, trout seem to enjoy eating adult caddisflies just about whenever they can get them.

Patterns: Deerhair Caddis, Elkhair Caddis, Colorado King, Henryville Special

Presentations:
As you present a caddis dry fly, remember that adult caddisflies (and most other aquatic insects) are active creatures. Seldom do they hold absolutely still as they drift on the water, so use your fly rod and line to give slight, occasional movement to the drifting fly. Two fine old presentation techniques, dapping and skittering, are usually overlooked, although they are especially well suited to fishing surface caddisfly imitations. Many times, caddis seem to be running on the water's surface, and often in opposition to the currents too. To skitter an adult caddis imitation, the fly should be placed downstream from you. Keep the fly line taut and the rod tip high. Rapidly strip in a few inches of line and the fly will flutter upstream on the water. Alternately, quickly raise the rod tip just a few inches and the fly will "jump" upstream. Then allow the fly to drift back downstream for a few inches and repeat the process. The largely forgotten skill of dapping involves two elements central to fly fishing: concealing the angler and tantalizing the trout. Use the cover of foliage or rocks to remain out of the trout's view. (Dapping experts sometimes hide themselves in trees overhanging the water.) From your place of concealment, reach out toward the water with your fly rod and let the fly (not the tippet, leader, or line) touch the water. Raise the fly from the water for a second or two, then allow the fly to alight and perhaps move a bit on the water once more. When dapping or skittering a fly, use a tippet of 4X or greater to avoid break-offs.

Colorado King Recipe

Hook: Dry-fly hook, sizes #16 to #10.
Thread: Black.
Tails: Two strands of peccary or boar bristle, spread widely.
Body: Yellow dubbing palmer-hackled with grizzly.
Wing: Deer hair or elk hair.

Comments:

The Colorado King can be a devastating imitation of the larger Front Range caddisflies.

The Deerhair Caddis and Elkhair Caddis are also popular and productive surface adult caddis patterns. However, deer-hair and elk-hair qualities (color, texture, and buoyancy, for example) can be virtually identical to one another, depending upon factors such as the part of the animal's body from which the hair was taken and the time of year when the animal was killed. Therefore, the two imitations are treated here as though they were the same pattern. Although only the Deerhair Caddis will be referenced, an Elkhair Caddis may be used in its place. Unless specified otherwise, the patterns should be brown-hackled.

A handful of other surface adult caddis patterns also deserve attention. Through several generations of Front Range fly fishing, the Trude, Rio Grande King, and Western Coachman have earned reputations as premium caddis dry flies. With their awkwardly proportioned bodies and white calf-tail wings, these three flies may defy the logic of seemingly more "realistic" caddis patterns, but they can raise trout when nothing else will work. They're also easy to see. You may want to select one as your adult caddis imitation of last (or first) resort. The Goddard Caddis, King's River Caddis, and Fluttering Caddis are regionally popular as well.

The Spent Adult Caddis—Like mayfly spinners, some caddisflies (such as the American grannom) become exhausted after laying eggs. Spent caddisflies drifting on the water's surface make easy, appealing targets for trout, but anglers seldom possess an appropriate imitation.

Pattern: Lawson's Spent Partridge Caddis

Presentations:
Dead drifts work best. When possible, cast to rising fish.

Lawson's Spent Partridge Caddis Recipe
Hook: Dry-fly hook, sizes #18 to #12.
Thread: Black.
Body: Brown-olive fur dubbing.
Wing: Partridge fibers.
Head: Peacock herl overwound with brown hackle, trimmed flush with the fly's top and bottom.

Comments:
This is also an exceptionally fine pattern for imitating small caddisflies, especially in low or calm waters.

Notes on the Top Ten Front Range Caddisflies
In the fly-angling world, caddisflies have been studied seriously for only about twenty years. In contrast, the activities and habits of mayflies have been observed and documented for centuries. Therefore, the particular times of day when a caddisfly might emerge or lay eggs still cannot be predicted with much accuracy. However, it's worth noting that as a rule, caddisflies

become more active later in the day as the weather grows warmer. For example, a hatch of a particular caddisfly that occurs during the morning in early May might take place in the afternoon in early July, or in the evening in mid-August. Five of the top ten caddisflies are especially numerous in streams and rivers at elevations above 8,000 feet. These high-mountain caddis include the little autumn stream sedge, tan short-horn sedge, green sedge, big gray spotted sedge, and pale western stream sedge. They also commonly occur in lower altitudes.

When tied in appropriate size and color, any of the recommended dry-fly patterns listed in Figure 4 might be used successfully to imitate nearly any Front Range surface adult caddisfly. In sizes #16 and smaller, the Deerhair Caddis and Henryville Special are often tied without palmer-hackle (the feather that is wound in a spiral around a fly's body). If a caddis dry fly rides too high on the water, trim the lower portions of the fly's hackle so that they're flush with the underside of the fly's body. Never be reluctant to alter *any* fly (no matter how crude your in-the-field modifications may appear) if you believe you might improve its performance. Further observations on the insects follow; see also Figures 3 (page 22) and 4 (page 23).

Little autumn stream sedge (Philopotamidae: *Wormaldia gabriella*)—This is one of the first and last caddisflies to emerge during the course of the Front Range caddisfly season. A ginger-hackled Henryville Special tied with a peacock-herl body makes a particularly effective imitation of the adult.

Tan short-horn sedge (Glossosomatidae: *Glossosoma* sp.)—The adult has antennae barely as long as its body. Trout feed ravenously upon the insect's periodically drifting larvae.

American grannom (Brachycentridae: *Brachycentrus* sp.)—As an imitation of the surface-drifting adult, a Deerhair Caddis can work best when tied with a bright green floss body. Spent adults are common after the insect has laid eggs.

Little spotted sedge (Hydropsychidae: *Cheumatopsyche* sp.)—A hatch often begins subtly and slowly, with just a few of the newly emerged adults apparent in the air and around the water. The initial emergence stages of this drab, diminutive insect are usually overlooked by anglers, but not by trout. Sparse hatches of the little spotted sedge often precede or follow the more substantial ones.

Green sedge (Rhyacophilidae: *Rhyacophila* sp.)—The most prominent of Front Range caddisflies. Its uncased larvae abound in riffles. Hatches and egg-laying occur from spring to autumn.

Spotted sedge (Hydropsychidae: *Hydropsyche* sp.)—Compared to other caddis, the emerging pupae of the spotted sedge usually remain in the water for the longest periods of time, often drifting in or near to the surface film.

Long-horn sedge (Leptoceridae: *Oecetis* sp.)—The antennae of the adult are the most lengthy of any regional caddisfly, about a third longer than the insect's body. Ideally, the adult is imitated by a Colorado King. If another pattern is used, its hackling should be light-colored, either ginger or grizzly. Watch for this caddis around slow and still waters.

Big gray spotted sedge (Hydropsychidae: *Arctopsyche grandis*)—The appearance of this caddis signals some of the best dry-fly fishing opportunities in the Front Range. The heaviest hatches usually occur between mid-July and mid-August.

Little plain brown sedge (Lepidostomatidae: *Lepidostoma* sp.)—Dry-fly imitations should be ginger-hackled. Depending on its species, the insect might lay eggs near or on shore.

Pale western stream sedge (Limnephilidae: *Chyranda centralis*)—Though one of the region's larger caddisflies, the insect frequently appears in small streams. The larva is about twice the size of the adult.

Other Front Range Caddisflies

Microcaddis (Hydroptilidae: *Hydroptila* sp.)—This tiny (sizes #24 to #20) caddis generally prefers a sandy or weedy streambed. The insect's mid-June to September emergences are most noticeable on slack waters. Body colors of adults and pupae include shades of green, gray, tan, yellow, and orange. The insect's wings are usually gray or tan. Useful patterns include the Brassy, Spent Partridge Caddis, and soft-hackle flies. The mature larva builds a minuscule "purse-case" shelter of silk and fine sand that is shaped somewhat like a handbag or an elongated potato.

Summer flyer sedge (Limnephilidae: *Limnephilus* sp.)—A tube-case caddis, the summer flyer favors slow-moving sections of streams and rivers, and also lives in lakes and ponds. Emergences occur from July to September. In all its life stages, the insect's dominant color is reddish brown. The adult measures from 13 to 20 mm long (hook sizes #12 to #10), and its larva is about twice that size. Females lay eggs on shore. Emerging pupae either rise to the water's surface or crawl onto shoreline rocks and plants.

Brown checkered summer sedge (Polycentropodidae: *Polycentropus* sp.)—Emergences take place from mid-June to August. The habitat of this net-spinning caddis includes slow and still waters. The larva, pupa, and adult share the same body color: brown tinged with yellow. Adults are 8 to 10 mm long (hook sizes #18 to #16). Females lay eggs underwater.

Little black sedge (Philopotamidae: *Chimarra utahensis*)—A net-spinning caddis, the little black sedge is found in larger streams and rivers, where it emerges from May to early July. Its most successful adult imitation is the King's River Caddis (sizes #20 to #18), a pattern that replicates the insect's nearly black body and wings. Females lay their eggs underwater, and mature pupae crawl out of the water to emerge. The larvae build tapering, cylindrical silken nets (called "finger nets") that retain their shapes only while underwater.

Giant orange sedge (Limnephilidae: *Dicosmoecus* sp.)—The adult of this tube-case caddis often attains a length of 30 mm, which is about 1.25 inches. The larva is even bigger, the better part of 2 inches long. Emergences are infrequent but they are memorable. The adult is best imitated with a large Sofa Pillow (which suggests the insect's rusty-red body and gray wings).

FRONT RANGE MAYFLIES

Mayflies form one of the largest groups of aquatic insects in the Front Range. They typically measure from 4 to 14 mm long (hook sizes #24 to #10), exclusive of tails, and their prevalent body colors are some shade of brown or olive. Emergences begin in March and end around ice-in. Though some species are widespread throughout North America, others inhabit Rocky Mountain waters almost exclusively. For additional quick-reference information, see the following: Figures 5 (Emergences of Top Ten Front Range Mayflies), 6 (Top Ten Front Range Mayflies and Their Primary Imitations), 7 (Water Types Inhabited by Top Ten Front Range Mayflies), and 8 (Emergences and Spinner Falls of Top Ten Front Range Mayflies). From a fly

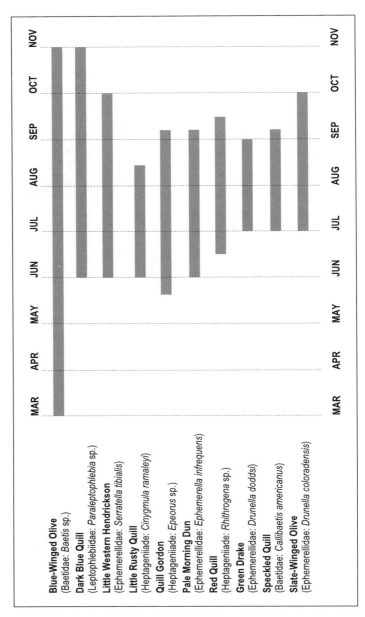

Blue-Winged Olive
(Baetidae: *Baetis* sp.)

Dark Blue Quill
(Leptophlebiidae: *Paraleptophlebia* sp.)

Little Western Hendrickson
(Ephemerellidae: *Serratella tibialis*)

Little Rusty Quill
(Heptageniiade: *Cinygmula ramaleyi*)

Quill Gordon
(Heptageniiade: *Epeorus* sp.)

Pale Morning Dun
(Ephemerellidae: *Ephemerella infrequens*)

Red Quill
(Heptageniiade: *Rhithrogena* sp.)

Green Drake
(Ephemerellidae: *Drunella doddsi*)

Speckled Quill
(Baetidae: *Callibaetis americanus*)

Slate-Winged Olive
(Ephemerellidae: *Drunella coloradensis*)

Fig. 5. Emergences of the Top Ten Front Range Mayflies

Mayflies:

Life-Stage Imitations:	Nymph			Emerger					Dun					Spinner		Size	Adult Color	Nymph Color	Category
	Pheasant Tail	RS-2	C.O. Gordon	Hare's Ear	Partridge-and-Orange	Wet Cahill	Natant Nymph	RS-2	Cahill	Quill Gordon	Comparadun	Adams	Blue-Winged Olive	Rusty-Brown Spinner	Quill-Body Spinner				
Blue-Winged Olive (Baetidae: *Baetis* sp.)	■	■			■	■	■	■			■	■	■	■		#24 to #14 (4 to 9mm)	Light to dark rusty-brown; blue-gray wings	Olive or rusty-brown	Swimmer
Dark Blue Quill (Leptophlebiidae: *Paraleptophlebia* sp.)		■		■		■	■	■	■	■		■	■	■		#18 to #14 (7 to 9mm)	Brown; slate wings	Yellow-brown	Crawler
Little Western Hendrickson (Ephemerellidae: *Serratella tibialis*)		■			■	■	■	■	■			■		■		#18 to #16 (7 to 8mm)	Dark rusty-brown; gray wings	Dark rusty-brown	Crawler
Little Rusty Quill (Heptageniidae: *Cinygmula ramaleyi*)	■	■	■		■	■	■	■	■	■		■		■		#18 to #16 (7 to 8mm)	Ringed rusty-brown; gray wings	Brown	Clinger
Quill Gordon (Heptageniidae: *Epeorus* sp.)		■	■		■	■	■	■	■	■		■		■		#16 to #12 (9 to 11mm)	Olive-gray to yellow; tan to gray wings	Light to dark brown	Clinger
Pale Morning Dun (Ephemerellidae: *Ephemerella infrequens*)	■	■	■	■	■	■	■	■			■	■	■	■	■	#18 to #14 (7 to 9mm)	Yellow-olive; gray wings	Yellow-brown	Crawler
Red Quill (Heptageniidae: *Rhithrogena* sp.)		■			■	■	■	■	■	■		■		■		#16 to #12 (8 to 13mm)	Olive or rusty-brown, ringed; gray or slate wings	Medium to dark olive; pale olive underside	Clinger
Green Drake (Ephemerellidae: *Drunella doddsi*)				■		■	■	■			■	■	■	■		#12 to #10 (12 to 14mm)	Dark olive; gray wings	Dark olive	Crawler
Speckled Quill (Callibaetidae: *Callibaetis americanus*)	■					■	■	■	■			■			■	#18 to #16 (7 to 8mm)	Brown-ringed gray; speckled gray wings	Brown	Swimmer
Slate-Winged Olive (Ephemerellidae: *Drunella coloradensis*)				■		■	■	■			■	■	■	■		#14 to #12 (9 to 12mm)	Dark olive; slate wings	Brown	Crawler

Fig. 6. The Top Ten Front Range Mayflies and Their Primary Imitations

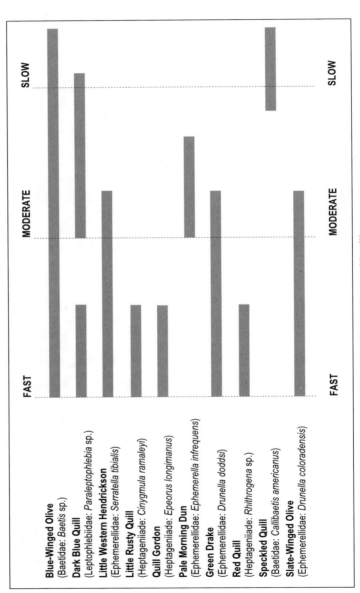

Fig. 7. Water Types Inhabited by the Top Ten Front Range Mayflies

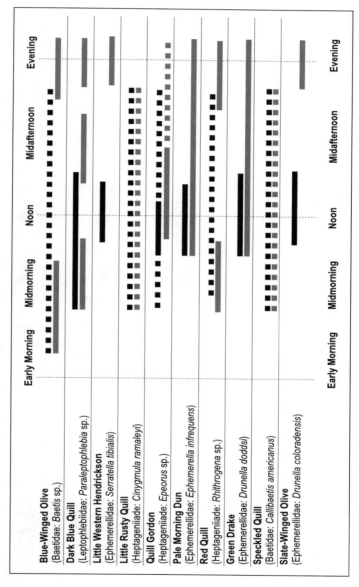

Fig. 8. Emergences and Spinner Falls of the Top Ten Front Range Mayflies

angler's perspective, the insect undergoes four important life stages: nymph, emerger, dun, and spinner. Though an adult mayfly might live from just a few hours to as long as a few weeks, most of a mayfly's one- to two-year life span is spent beneath the water's surface as a nymph.

Mayfly Life Stages and Imitations

The Mayfly Nymph—Most Front Range mayfly nymphs live in streambeds composed of rock, gravel, or sand, though a few varieties prefer a silty or weedy environment. Observing a mayfly nymph reveals a surprising amount of information regarding the insect in all its life stages. You can apply this knowledge both to your selection of mayfly life-stage imitations and the ways in which you fish them. Based upon the characteristics of its nymphs, nearly any Front Range mayfly falls into one of three categories: swimmer, clinger, or crawler. Look for the nymphs on or under the streambed, or find them as they drift or swim in the water. During a mayfly hatch, watch for recently cast-off nymphal cases (also called "shucks") in the calmer flows of a stream and along its shorelines. Although empty, a shuck can serve as a full-body "life mask" of the nymph that emerged from it. For purposes of basic identification, you can consider a nymph and its shuck as the same object. To determine a nymph's category, take a close look at the general shape of its body. You may need to use a small magnifier. Regardless, categorizing the insects takes a little practice. However, the more mayfly nymphs you observe and compare, the more adept you'll become at discerning the fundamental structural differences between them.

Swimmer nymphs. Prominent regional mayfly swimmers include the blue-winged olive (Baetidae: *Baetis* sp.) and the speckled quill (Baetidae: *Callibaetis* sp.).

You'll find the blue-winged olive in both moving and still waters. The speckled quill inhabits the slower flows of rivers and streams; it also occurs near shorelines of lakes and beaver ponds. The streamlined nymphs of both mayflies propel themselves by swimming. The wiggling motions of a mayfly swimmer nymph, along with its periodic behavioral drift, make it a favorite prey of trout. Behavioral drift (also known as "invertebrate drift") commonly occurs among aquatic insects. The term refers to a phenomenon during which large numbers of nymphs or larvae simultaneously release themselves from their streambed homes and then drift unrestrained in the currents. The event most often takes place in the early morning and late evening.

Patterns: Pheasant Tail, American Pheasant Tail, RS-2

Presentations:
An imitation is usually fished in an upstream or downstream presentation. Make the fly "swim" in 1- to 4-inch-long bursts by occasionally twitching the rod tip or stripping line.

Pattern Notes:
Popular colors for the thread thorax of a Pheasant Tail include brown, olive, yellow, orange, or red. The American Pheasant Tail has a peacock herl thorax, and in sizes #18 and larger may also have partridge fiber "legs." Both patterns are sometimes tied with olive- or yellow-dyed pheasant tail fibers. In addition, the flies often incorporate "flashback" wing cases (made of Krystal Flash or Flashabou), brass-bead heads, or both.

Rim Chung's RS-2 features a compact, tightly dubbed, beaver-fur body (either naturally colored or dyed olive or brown).The fly's wing case might be made from a clump of soft feathers or a short length of dark Antron yarn. Two Micro Fibbets or beaver guard-hairs serve as tails.

Clinger nymphs. Prominent regional mayfly clingers include the little rusty quill (Heptageniiade: *Cinygmula rama-*  *leyi*); quill gordon (Heptageniiade: *Epeorus* sp.); and red quill (Heptageniiade: *Rhithrogena* sp.). The flattened body of a clinger nymph helps the insect withstand the force of currents in its fast-water habitat. For identification purposes, note that the head of a clinger nymph is at least as wide as the broadest part of the insect's body. An inferior swimmer, a clinger nymph rarely surrenders its firm grip upon the streambed until the insect prepares to emerge.

Patterns: C.Q. Gordon, Hare's Ear

Presentation:
For a few days prior to emergence, mature clinger nymphs move into shallows that adjoin deeper, faster-running waters. As the nymphs move about searching for food, currents often knock them into the flows. Present an imitation nymph in a dead drift, in or just downstream of the areas where the nymphs have migrated.

Pattern Notes:
If you use a Hare's Ear to imitate a clinger nymph, you should trim or flatten the underside of its thorax. However, the C.Q. Gordon, developed by Eric Neufeld of Boulder, Colorado, is a better imitation.

C.Q. Gordon Recipe
Hook: Dry-fly hook, sizes #18 to #12.
Thread: Black.
Tail: Several pheasant-tail fibers.
Abdomen: Brown ostrich herl ribbed with brown goose biot or Larva Lace.
Thorax: Peacock herl.
Wingcase: Pheasant tail.
Legs: Partridge fibers.

Crawler nymphs. Prominent regional mayfly crawlers include the slate-winged olive (Ephemerellidae: *Drunella coloradensis*); green drake (Ephemerellidae: *Drunella doddsi*); little western hendrickson (Ephemerellidae: *Serratella tibialis*);

pale morning dun (Ephemerellidae: *Ephemerella infrequens*); dark blue quill (Leptophlebiidae: *Paraleptophlebia heteronea*). Most crawlers inhabit moderate- to fast-flowing waters. Com-

pared to clingers, crawlers have much more amply formed bodies and noticeably smaller heads. As they crawl along subsurface rocks and vegetation, the nymphs commonly get washed into the currents. They drift helplessly as they wait to regain their place on the streambed.

Pattern: Hare's Ear

Presentations:
Dead-drift presentations work best, though you'll need to adjust the fly's depth. A deeply drifted imitation can be the most productive. However, preemergent crawler nymphs gather in slow-moving waters and begin a series of attempts to reach the surface. The insect may repeatedly ascend, descend, and drift at varying levels above the streambed. At these times, use up-and-across presentations, occasionally raising and lowering the rod tip so the drifting fly alternately rises and falls.

Pattern Notes:
Like the Pheasant Tail, the Hare's Ear has its popular options, including a flashback wing case, bead head, and a choice of body color (usually brown or dark olive), to which tyers sometimes add highlights of gray, light brown, or yellow. A soft, flexible tail (made of a few fibers of pheasant tail or mallard flank feather) can improve the fly's effectiveness, especially in size #16 and smaller. In addition, a single strand of Krystal Flash is often tied in together with the fly's gold or copper wire ribbing.

The Mayfly Emerger—When mature, the typical mayfly nymph prepares to leave the streambed and to shed its nymphal case. During this process, the mayfly is called an emerger. Factors affecting mayfly emergences include winds, currents, water and air temperatures, and the size and strength of the emerging insects. With so many variables to consider during a mayfly emergence, don't hesitate to take a quick break from fishing. Do you see the bulging or boiling riseforms that signal the presence of emerger-eating trout? Or do you notice flashes of trout moving as the fish pick off emergers in deeper waters? Can you locate mayflies rising from the water's surface? Perhaps you can see the duns themselves drifting on the water or flying through the air. Look for them on your shirtsleeve and on your waders. Are there any mayfly nymphs or shucks floating near the shoreline or around branches, rocks, bridges, or other objects that protrude from the streambed? With careful observation and luck, you'll learn not only about the emergers' physical appearance but their behavior too.

Patterns: Partridge-and-Orange, Wet Cahill, Natant Nymph, Parachute Emerger, and RS-2

Presentations:
Whether you fish up- or down and across-stream, the key to a successful presentation often lies in being able to determine at what depth the natural insects are emerging. For example, mayfly swimmers break free of their shucks while on or near the water's surface. Some mayfly clingers emerge while on or near the streambed, others while close to or on the surface. Nearly all mayfly crawlers leave their shucks well before they reach the water's surface.

Wet Cahill Recipe
Hook: Dry-fly hook, sizes #18 to #10.
Thread: Black.
Tail: Brown or furnace hackle fibers.
Body: Olive-brown fur ribbed with gold wire.

Wing: Mallard flank.
Beard: Brown or furnace hackle fibers.

Comments:
For an old-fashioned fly of the British Isles, the Wet Cahill seems exceptionally well adapted to catching Colorado trout, whether the pattern is fished deep or in the film. Traditionally, the fly is tied with wings that are a bit longer than its body, but shortening them sometimes enhances the Wet Cahill's effectiveness as an emerger.

Natant Nymph Recipe
Hook: Dry-fly hook, sizes #20 to #12.
Thread: Black, brown, or gray.
Tail: Grouse or hackle fibers; optional.
Body: Fur dubbing, color to suit.
Wingcase: Polypropylene yarn.
Parachute hackle: Dun or grizzly.

Comments:
Credit for creation of the Natant Nymph (also called the Floating Nymph) goes to the late Charlie Brooks. Brooks recommended that a piece of nylon stocking be used to enclose the poly-yarn wingcase. The fly can represent a surface-emerging mayfly (such as a blue-winged olive) or nearly any other type of mayfly that has been unable to escape its nymphal shuck.

Befus Parachute Emerger Recipe

Hook:	Dry-fly hook, sizes #24 to #16.
Thread:	Gray.
Tail:	Orange Antron or Z-Lon.
Body:	Olive-dyed muskrat.
Wingcase:	Closed-cell foam.
Parachute hackle:	Medium dun.
Head area:	Natural muskrat.

Comments:

The Parachute Emerger was developed by Brad Befus, of Boulder, Colorado. In imitation of a pale morning dun, the pattern can also be tied with a sulphur-yellow muskrat body. The fly is extremely effective in hook sizes #18 to #22.

When weighted, an RS-2 can serve as an imitation of a subsurface mayfly emerger. With floatant applied to its body or wing, the pattern can also be presented so that it drifts in or near the surface film.

The Mayfly Dun—Once rid of its shuck, a newly emerged mayfly unfolds and dries its wings as it drifts on the water. The mayfly has become a dun, a sexually immature but otherwise fully formed adult mayfly. The length of time that a dun might remain on the water usually varies according to the mayfly's category. A mayfly crawler dun (such as a pale morning dun) exhibits the longest-lasting drifts. A mayfly clinger dun departs the water's surface more quickly, and a mayfly swimmer dun spends the least time on the water before flying away.

Patterns: Quill Gordon, Cahill, No-Hackle
Comparadun, Adams, Blue-Winged Olive

Presentations:
Successful presentations of a dun imitation are most often up-and-across-stream. Drag-free drifts are usually desirable, but never hesitate to impart slight action to the fly, especially if no trout have risen to it.

Pattern Notes:
The best body colors for a Cahill include light or dark rust-brown, dark olive, and yellow-olive. The No-Hackle Compara-dun is usually reserved for fishing calm flows, but it also produces well in fast waters. When tied with a dark body, the Blue-Winged Olive is also popular as an imitation of the Dark Blue Quill. When duns become active on moderate- to fast-flowing waters, sometimes there's no substitute for a high-floating dry fly such as a Gray Wulff, Royal Wulff, or Humpy.

The Mayfly Spinner—A spinner is a sexually mature mayfly. After spinners mate, the females alight on the water to lay eggs and die. Their final return to the water is known as a "spinner fall." The two spinner forms of most interest to trout are those that are in or near a state of complete physical collapse. A half-spent spinner holds its wings slightly angled up from its body; the wings of a fully spent spinner spread out from the body's sides and rest upon the water.

Presentations:
Because spinner imitations are often fished in low-light conditions, and because trout often take the natural insects in a subdued manner, using an indicator on your leader can be helpful in detecting strikes. A small, wispy piece of yarn (treated with floatant, if necessary) can be attached to the leader with a slip knot placed about 2 to 3 feet above the fly. The yarn indicator is visible, lightweight, and rarely spooks fish.

Patterns: Rusty Spinner, Quill-Body Spinner

Pattern Notes:
If one wing of a fully spent spinner pattern is made to tilt a bit upward from the fly's body, the pattern can serve as a worthwhile

imitation of either spinner form. You can obtain this effect by repeatedly stroking and pulling up on one wing of the fly, though it's preferable that the fly be tied initially with one wing slightly elevated. The dubbed thorax of a quill-bodied spinner should be rust-brown or yellow-olive.

Notes on the Top Ten Front Range Mayflies
(See also Figures 5, 6, 7, and 8, pages 36–39.)

Blue-winged olive—The most prolific of regional mayflies, the insect ranges in length from 4 to 9 mm (hook sizes #24 to #14). Duns vary in body coloration from light to dark reddish- or rust-brown. Nymphs abound in riffles.

Dark blue quill—This mayfly has two species: *heteronea* and *debilis*. Although the two appear to be identical, *heteronea* is a fast-water mayfly and usually emerges from June to August. In contrast, *debilis* inhabits slow to moderate flows and emerges later in the season, usually between August and October. Emergences of both species generally occur close to shorelines.

Pale morning dun—Two species exist. *Ephemerella infrequens* inhabits moderate flows and emerges from June to early September. *Ephemerella inermis* is similarly colored but smaller (5 to 7 mm long; hook sizes #22 to #18). *Inermis* lives in nearly all types of moving water and emerges from July to August in the Front Range.

Speckled quill—Two common species of the speckled quill differ in size, coloration, and emergence periods. *Callibaetis americanus* has a brown-ringed gray body and speckled gray wings. It ranges in size from 7 to 8 mm (hook sizes #18 to #16). The mayfly begins and ends its emergences a few weeks earlier than a larger species, *Callibaetis pallidus*, which measures from 8 to 9 mm long (hook sizes #16 to #14). A *pallidus* dun has a light brown body and yellow wings. Duns of both species usually have undersides tinged with yellow or tan.

Green drake and **slate-winged olive**—These mayflies often hatch concurrently, their duns lingering on the water for long periods of time.

Little western hendrickson—Emergences and spinner falls are frequently masked by the activities of other, more conspicuous aquatic insects.

Red quill and **quill gordon**—Found in few other places in the world, these mayflies thrive at high elevation fast waters.

Little rusty quill—The mayfly lives primarily in streams at elevations between 8,000 and 11,000 feet. Its emergences and spinner falls tend to be eclipsed by the activity of other insects.

Other Front Range Mayflies

Though not nearly as prominent as the mayflies discussed earlier, the following mayflies sometimes play a significant role in Front Range fly fishing.

Trico (Tricorythidae: *Tricorythodes minutus*)—Sizable emergences occur mostly in sections of the South Platte and Cache la Poudre rivers. Spinner falls of early- and late-morning hours can offer fine fishing opportunities. These dark-bodied mayflies measure just 3 to 6 mm long (hook sizes #28 to #20) and prefer silty-bottomed, slow-moving waters.

Gray fox or **pale evening dun** (Heptageniiade: *Heptagenia solitaria*)—Emergences begin around mid-July and last about eight weeks. The insects range in size from 8 to 10 mm long (hook sizes #16 to #14). The nymph has a light- to dark-olive body and is best imitated by a Hare's Ear. An Adams or Cahill can approximate' the dun, whose body is grayish-yellow. For a spinner pattern, select a Ginger Quill Spinner.

Western green drake (Ephemerellidae: *Drunella grandis*)—The western green drake has a much stronger presence in Colorado's Western Slope rivers. It emerges only sporadically (from June to July) in Front Range waters. The adult (12 to 16 mm long; hook sizes #12 to #10) is distinguished by a brown-ringed green body.

Brown drake (Siphlonuridae: *Ameletus* sp.)—At elevations above 7,000 feet, *Ameletus* populates most fast waters of the Front Range. However, the mayflies are as mysterious as they are numerous: Their matings, emergences, and spinner falls remain largely undocumented. The nymph and adult measure from 10 to 14 mm long (hook sizes #14 to #10) and hatches occur from ice-out to ice-in. In all life phases, *Ameletus* body coloration ranges from reddish-brown to olive to dingy yellow. The *Ameletus* nymph, an agile swimmer, can be imitated with a Pheasant Tail.

Great red quill (Ephemerellidae: *Timpanoga hecuba*)—Where waters flow at a slow to moderate rate, emergences occasionally occur from July to August. The adult (which has a light- and dark-brown body and gray wings) measures from 14 to 16 mm long (hook sizes #12 to #10). It's best imitated by a Quill Gordon.

White mayfly (Polymitarcyidae: *Ephoron album*)— Ephoron is a slow-water mayfly. Until ready to emerge, nymphs remain beneath silt or similar material into which they've burrowed. Duns and spinners have grayish-white bodies and pale gray wings. Adults measure from 10 to 12 mm long (hook sizes #14 to #12).

Tiny whitewinged sulphur (Caenidae: *Caenis bajaensis*)— This buff-colored insect is about 3 mm long (hook sizes #30 to #28) and lives only a few hours. Often mistaken for a midge, it hatches in midsummer in backwaters and beaver ponds.

FRONT RANGE MIDGES

Whatever the time of year, no matter how subdued the activities of insects and fish may appear, chances are trout are eating midges. Virtually every Front Range water that holds trout also supports substantial midge populations. Some of the world's most hardy and adaptable aquatic insects, they emerge throughout the year, even in midwinter, as long as at least a bit of water remains ice-free. In January and February, when daytime air temperatures are often below 32 degrees Fahrenheit, a midge hatch might take place in a particular water just once in twenty-four hours, usually between late morning and early afternoon. As the weather grows warmer, the same water may produce a half-dozen or more midge emergences daily. The specific times of day during which these emergences occur are generally unpredictable.

As a larva, pupa, or adult, a midge might measure from 1 to 15 mm long (hook sizes #32 to #10), though the most prevalent Front Range midges are from 3 to 7 mm long (hook sizes #28 to #18). The tube-shaped body of a midge larva or pupa is often tinged with black, red, green, or orange. The adult midge is distinguished by its long legs, feathery antennae, and lack of tails. Its dominant body color is commonly a shade of olive, green, brown, or gray. In general, the adult forms of a midge and a mosquito resemble each another, although Front Range midges neither bite nor sting. Probably more than 1,000 midge species exist, but few have been classified by entomologists. For this reason, midge identification seldom progresses beyond the

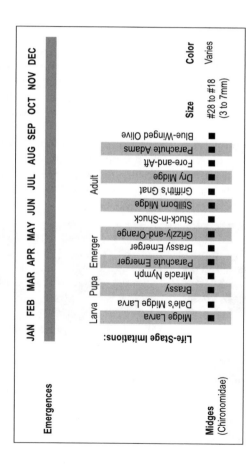

Fig. 9. Emergences and Imitations of Front Range Midges

family level of Chironomidae. Midges are often referred to as chironomids. See Figure 9 (Emergences and Imitations of Front Range Midges).

Midge Life Stages and Imitations

The Midge Larva—The worm-like larvae can survive nearly anywhere on the bottom of a stream or pond, though heavy concentrations of them often live upon submerged branches and vegetation. In addition, the larvae sometimes drift freely in both still and moving waters.

Patterns: Midge Larva, Dale's Midge Larva

Presentations:
Generally, a larval imitation should be presented in a dead drift. However, a trout rarely moves far to feed on something as small and commonplace as a larval chironomid. Fish the imitation carefully and thoroughly so it drifts through nearly every cubic inch of a likely holding area. This painstaking approach becomes even more important when fishing in the icy waters of winter and early spring. A midge larva fly can also be effective when tied as a dropper to a larger subsurface pattern (such as a Prince Nymph) or to a dry fly or emerger (such as a Stimulator or Parachute Emerger).

Dale's Midge Larva Recipe
Hook: Dry-fly hook, sizes #26 to #18.
Thread: Black (or other color to match the color of the natural insect).

Body: A few fibers of mallard flank wound along the hook shank.

Rib: Gold or copper wire.

Comments:

Developed by Dale Darling of Longmont, Colorado, this simple fly rates as one of the best midge patterns around.

The Midge Pupa—A midge larva develops into a pupa that remains dormant for several days beneath the streambed or within a cocoon. The fully mature pupa then swims to the water's surface to emerge. An imitation of a midge pupa resembles that of a midge larva, but it includes a thorax, tailing, or both.

Patterns: Brassy, Miracle Nymph

Presentations:

In the first stages of a midge emergence, trout focus on eating the ascending, swimming pupae. Down-and-across presentations are often most productive. You'll probably need to adjust the amount and placement of weight (if any) clinched onto your tippet in order to place the artificial fly at the depth of the natural insects.

Miracle Nymph Recipe

Hook: Dry-fly hook, sizes #24 to #18.

Thread: Black.

Abdomen: White floss ribbed with gold or copper wire.

Thorax: Muskrat.

The Midge Emerger—Midges hatch in the calmer flows of moving waters; in still waters, emergences may occur near or far from shore. The emergence process of midges is similar to that of mayfly swimmers (such as the blue-winged olive), but can last longer.

A fully mature midge pupa swims quickly to the water's surface, where the insect begins to emerge from an opening in the end of its pupal shuck. The shuck is roughly tubular, usually light amber in color, and about as long as the adult insect. An emerging midge almost always remains attached to its shuck until its wings have dried and so cannot escape the water at will.

The combined length of a midge and its shuck is nearly twice that of the insect when it is fully developed. During a midge hatch (and often for a half-hour or so afterward), the midge emerger appeals to trout more than the smaller, less vulnerable midge adult.

Patterns: Parachute Emerger, Brassy Emerger,
        Grizzly-and-Orange, Stuck-in-Shuck,
        Hill's Stillborn Midge

Presentations:
Though a midge emerger imitation is usually presented in a dead drift, imparting a slight twitching motion to the fly can help induce a take. The fly should drift on or slightly below the water's surface.

Brassy Emerger Recipe
Hook: Dry-fly hook, sizes #20 to #16.
Thread: Black.

Abdomen: Copper wire wound two-thirds of the way up the hook shank.

Thorax: Two or three strands of peacock herl or ostrich herl.

Comments:

When both wire and herl are dressed with floatant, the fly rides on the water's surface. Apply a tiny amount of floatant just to the herl (or to the knot connecting the tippet to the fly), and the Brassy Emerger hangs in the surface film.

Grizzly-and-Orange Recipe

Hook: Dry-fly hook, sizes #18 to #14.
Thread: Black.
Body: Orange floss ribbed with gold wire.
Hackle: One to three turns of soft, grizzly hen hackle.

Comments:

The hackle should be only about half the length of the hook shank.

Stuck-in-Shuck Recipe

Hook:	Dry-fly hook, sizes #24 to #18.
Thread:	Gray.
Tail:	Several strands of orange Antron or Z-Lon.
Body:	Thread.
Overbody:	Several strands of white or gray Antron or Z-Lon.
Collar:	One or two strands of peacock herl.

Hill's Stillborn Midge Recipe

Hook:	Dry-fly hook, sizes #24 to #18.
Thread:	Black.
Body:	Thread.
Wing:	A tuft of muskrat fur tied onto the middle of the hook shank.
Hackle:	One or two turns of grizzly hackle.

Comments:
The hackle is the only part of the fly to which floatant should be applied.

 **The Midge Adult**—Trout feed on clusters of midges that gather on the water's surface to mate. Trout also rise to eat individual midge adults.

Patterns: Griffith's Gnat, Dry Midge, Parachute Adams, Blue-Winged Olive, Fore-and-Aft

Presentations:
Ideally, an artificial adult midge is offered in dead drift to rising fish, but delicately presenting the fly along the quiet, slack waters of a shoreline (where adult midges tend to congregate) can tempt some large trout. Sections of water that seem to offer the easiest wading may also hold the biggest fish. Even a 5-pound rainbow might rise to take a well-placed, size #26 midge dry fly.

Pattern Notes:
Adult midge imitations customarily work best when tied with dark bodies. Choose a Griffith's Gnat or Fore-and-Aft when trout are rising to midge clusters. The Dry Midge is essentially a Cahill-style dry fly tied without wings.

FRONT RANGE STONEFLIES

The cold, well-oxygenated, and rocky waters of Front Range streams and rivers create a near-perfect habitat for stoneflies. Exclusive of their tails and antennae, these prolific insects vary in size from 7 to 35 mm long (hook sizes #18 to #4). Though stonefly hatches may occur throughout most of the year, the most important emergences begin in March and end by late October. A stonefly spends much of its one- to three-year life as a subsurface nymph. Nymphs and adults of the same species are about equal in size. Just five principal kinds of stoneflies live in the Front Range region. See Figures 10 (Emergences of the Top Five Front Range Stoneflies) and 11 (Top Five Front Range Stoneflies and Their Primary Imitations).

Stonefly Life Stages and Imitations

 **The Stonefly Nymph**—Most stonefly nymphs remain well secured in or on the streambed and seldom become available to trout until their emergence. During a

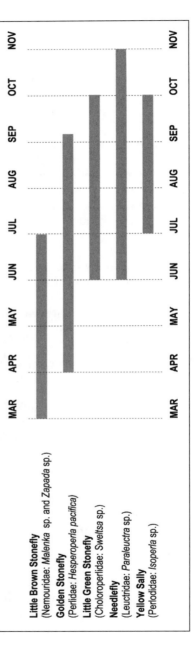

Fig. 10. Emergences of the Top Five Front Range Stoneflies

Stoneflies:	Nymph					Adult						Size	Adult Color	Nymph Color
Life-Stage Imitations:	Hare's Ear	American PT, Olive	American PT, Yellow	Orange Stone Nymph	20-Inch Nymph	Turkey Quill	Spent Partridge Caddis	Trude, Chartreuse	Colorado King	Sofa Pillow	Deer-Hair Caddis			
Little Brown Stonefly (Nemouridae: *Malenka* sp. and *Zapada* sp.)	■	■				■	■			■		#18 to #12 (7 to 12mm)	Dark brown to black body; gray wings	Dark brown to black
Golden Stonefly (Perlidae: *Hesperoperla pacifica*)	■		■	■	■				■		■	#10 to #4 (22 to 35mm)	Golden tan to dark brown body; tan to brown wings	Golden tan to dark brown
Little Green Stonefly (Choloroperlidae: *Sweltsa* sp.)								■	■			#16 to #14 (10 to 12mm)	Dull yellow to chartreuse body; yellow to pale green wings	Brown tinged with yellow
Needlefly (Leuctridae: *Paraleuctra* sp.)	■	■				■	■					#18 to #14 (7 to 12mm)	Dark brown body; tan to brown wings	Dark brown
Yellow Sally (Perlodidae: *Isoperla* sp.)	■		■						■		■	#18 to #12 (7 to 16mm)	Yellow-green body and wings	Drab yellow or green-brown

Fig. 11. The Top Five Front Range Stoneflies and Their Primary Imitations

hatch, nymphs drift into slack currents and crawl out of the water onto streambanks, plants, and rocks, where they split their shucks open and emerge. As an emergence progresses, trout become increasingly intent upon eating the drifting subsurface nymphs, only rarely showing interest in any adult stoneflies. Some smaller kinds of Front Range stonefly nymphs resemble the nymphs of mayflies.

Patterns: Hare's Ear, American Pheasant Tail (PT),
Orange Stone Nymph, 20-Inch Nymph

Presentations:
In riffled water, try casting the fly down- and across-stream. Use a stout tippet (4X or greater) and prepare for strong, sudden strikes. Deeply drifted presentations in and around pools and pocket water also produce well. During a stonefly emergence, present a nymph in a dead drift near the streambank or another area where the preemergent insects have gathered.

Pattern Notes:
When used as a stonefly nymph imitation, the American Pheasant Tail works most effectively when dyed olive or yellow.

Orange Stone Nymph Recipe
Hook: Wet-fly hook, 2X or 3X, sizes #12 to #8.
Thread: Black.
Tails: Two dark goose biots.
Abdomen: Orange floss ribbed with brown or black ostrich herl.

Thorax: Dark hare's ear dubbing palmered with brown hackle. A length of red yarn is tied beneath the thorax.

Wingcase: A section of dark gray goose wing quill.

Comments:
The Orange Stone Nymph is based on a hellgrammite pattern originated by Doug Prince (of Prince Nymph fame).

20-Inch Nymph Recipe
Hook: Wet-fly hook, 2X or 3X, sizes #12 to #8.
Thread: Black.
Tails: Two dark goose biots.
Abdomen: Peacock herl ribbed with copper wire and single-strand white floss.
Thorax: Medium-dark hare's ear dubbing. A section of brown hen hackle tied above the thorax creates the pattern's "legs."
Wingcase: Peacock herl.

The Adult Stonefly—Stoneflies routinely fall or are blown into the water, especially while trying to mate. Ovipositing female stoneflies alight on the water's surface to release their brightly colored eggs. In either circumstance, trout rise to feed upon the vulnerable adult insects—or a well-presented dry fly.

Patterns: Spent Partridge Caddis, Trude, Colorado King, DeerHair Caddis, Turkey Quill, Sofa Pillow

Presentations:
Present an adult stonefly pattern in much the same way you'd present a caddis dry fly. Because the natural insect is usually active, either laying eggs on the water or trying to escape it, remember to convey occasional movement to the drifting imitation. Dapping and skittering techniques (described on page 30 in Front Range Caddisflies) are also worthwhile.

Pattern Notes:
Make the Trude your first choice of dry fly for imitating an adult yellow sally or little green stonefly, especially when the insects are laying eggs.

Turkey Quill Recipe
Hook: Dry-fly hook, sizes #18 to #14.
Thread: Black.
Tail: Brown hackle fibers.
Body: Dark brown dubbing.
Wing(s): One or two sections of turkey quill tied in (narrow edge down) at a slight angle to the body.
Hackle: Two or three turns of brown hackle.

Comments:
The Turkey Quill is also productive when tied with an orange or green floss body. A splitting and fraying of the quill wing occurs after the pattern has hooked a few trout, but this seems only to enhance the fly's appeal. On average, a well-tied Turkey Quill endures about thirty hookups. The pattern casts easily, floats naturally, and catches even finicky trout in thin waters.

Sofa Pillow Recipe

Hook: Dry-fly hook, 1X or 2X, sizes #12 to #8.
Thread: Black.
Tail: Deer hair or red saddle hackle fibers.
Body: Orange floss.
Wing: Deer hair or squirrel hair.
Hackle: Brown, grizzly, or both.

Comments:

As an imitation of an adult golden stonefly, few flies compare with the Sofa Pillow, though an orange-bodied Stimulator makes an adequate substitute.

Notes on the Top Five Front Range Stoneflies
(See also Figures 10, page 58, and 11, page 59)

Little brown stonefly—Imitations of this delicate insect are most useful in sizes #18 and #16. Even early in the season, trout rise to little brown stones fluttering across shallow waters warmed by the sun.

Golden stonefly—Also known as the brown willow fly. Nymphs take as long as three years to mature. Found in moderately fast-moving waters, golden stonefly nymphs are exceptionally active and predatory feeders that frequently become dislodged from the stream bottom.

Little green stonefly—One of the area's most numerous stoneflies, the little green stonefly is common in high mountain streams.

Needlefly—Entomologists classify the needlefly as a "rolled-winged" stonefly. When not in flight, the insect holds its wings close to and rolled in toward its body. Anglers often mistake the needlefly for a small, narrow-winged moth.

Yellow sally—In fast-moving streams, the yellow sally may have as much or more presence than the little green stonefly. Because the nymphs of some yellow sally species are proficient swimmers and hunters, they represent a significant source of food to trout.

Front Range stonefly hatches are intermittent events and difficult to forecast. However, the following field observations might be helpful as a guide to the behavior of regional stoneflies. Early in the season, little brown stoneflies usually emerge and lay eggs around midday. In late spring and early summer, they might hatch and oviposit during nearly any daylight hour. From April through May, emergences and egg-laying activities of the golden stonefly occur mostly in the late morning or early afternoon. From June through September, though, the insect commonly emerges twice a day: once in the afternoon, and again around dusk or after dark. In the same months, the golden stonefly frequently lays eggs in the early morning and late afternoon. During the summer, the little green stonefly, needlefly, and yellow sally hatch and lay eggs at irregular intervals throughout the day and often well into the evening. By mid-September, the insects are active mainly in the early to midafternoon, and if air temperatures are warm, occasionally in the late afternoon and early evening.

Other Front Range Stoneflies

Winter Stonefly (Capniidae: *Capnia* sp.) and **Little Red Stonefly** (Taeniopterygidae)—These insects hatch from November to February, when waters are largely icebound and inaccessible. Body sizes of nymphs and adults range from 7 to 10 mm (hook sizes #18 to #16).

Early orange stonefly (Perlodidae: *Isogenoides* sp.)—The adult and nymph forms resemble those of the yellow sally, but they are larger (sizes #14 to #10) and tinged with orange. Small hatches occur from April to June.

Giant salmonfly (Pteronarcyidae: *Pteronarcys californica*)—Emergences are uncommon but sometimes take place during the warmest days of summer. The adult measures about 2 inches long.

FRONT RANGE TERRESTRIALS AND OTHER TROUT FOODS

Terrestrial (land-dwelling) insects and bugs become food for trout after they fall, jump, or otherwise accidentally arrive in the water. For quick reference, see Figure 12 (Front Range Terrestrials and Other Trout Foods: Their Sizes and Occurrences). Of the terrestrials found near Front Range waters, the three most important to fly fishing are grasshoppers, ants, and beetles.

Grasshoppers

In most parts of the country, grasshoppers are associated almost exclusively with autumn-season fly fishing. In Colorado's Front Range, however, grasshoppers are active and plentiful for about half the year, from April through much of October. Cool temperatures and overcast skies diminish grasshopper activity; warm days and bright sun increase it. In mountainous terrain, south-facing slopes often hold the largest, most energetic populations of the insects. Even at noon on a brilliantly sunny midsummer day, when all fish seem to have retreated to their hiding places, a well-placed hopper imitation can rouse the most careful trout into a violent strike. Grasshoppers are widespread, found mostly in grassy areas near ponds and streams at elevations up to around 10,000 feet. Crickets live in the region too, but not in such great numbers.

Patterns: Parachute Hopper, Joe's Hopper, Whitlock Hopper

Presentations:
A trout that rises to a big, splashy grasshopper is rarely leader-shy, but it can still be spooked by a fly line floating nearby. When casting a hopper, use a leader at least 8 feet long. You can fish hopper patterns successfully nearly anywhere, on moving or still water, but one of the best locations is close to shore, especially where banks are undercut and provide prime lies for trout. When possible, cast the fly so it lands on the bank or other place above and near the water (such as a streambed boulder). Then, with a quick twitch of the rod tip, "hop" the fly onto the water. Interrupt the fly's drift with small, rapid line-strips and rod movements.

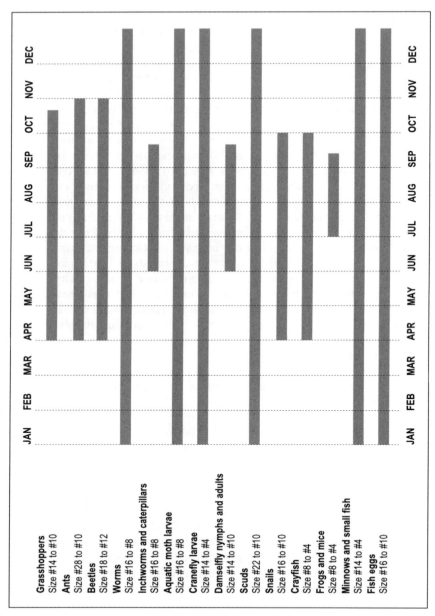

Fig. 12. Front Range Terrestrials and Other Trout Foods: Their Sizes and Occurrences

Pattern Notes:
Imitations are predominantly green, olive, or yellow. They're most often tied on 2X- or 3X-long hooks in sizes #14 to #10. If a pattern fails to produce, augment it with a small, subsurface dropper (such as a Partridge-and-Grizzly, Midge Larva, or Pheasant Tail) positioned about a foot below the dry fly.

Ants and Beetles
In the forests, meadows, and canyonlands adjoining Front Range streams and ponds, don't be surprised to see anthills over a foot high. Ants are some of the region's most plentiful terrestrial insects, typically measuring from 4 to 14 mm long (hook sizes #24 to #10). Some have red-and-black bodies, but most are black, brown, or cinnamon in color. Ants exist in such profusion it seems inevitable that so many of them end up awash in the drifts or floating on the water's surface and are devoured by trout. Ants first appear by early April and maintain a strong presence through late October. Terrestrial beetles are active during the same period, and as surface-drifting adult insects, they can be noteworthy trout foods too. Both ants and beetles are found at elevations up to 12,000 feet.

Patterns:
Productive ant imitations might be tied with foam, thread, or dubbed-fur bodies, but be sure to carry both dry- and wet-fly patterns. Dry-fly beetles made of foam, peacock herl, or dark-dyed deer hair are most effective.

Presentations:
In early to mid-August, flying ants (which can be imitated with standard ant patterns or with dark, caddis dry flies) often swarm around high mountain lakes, even at elevations above 11,000 feet. These events generate some of the most enjoyable (and easy) dry-fly fishing imaginable. Cast to rising trout if you like, but just get an ant pattern out onto the water. Let it lie motionless a few seconds, then quickly move it a half-inch or so, repeating the process until a trout strikes. If the technique fails, switch to a fly one or two sizes smaller, or pull the fly into the surface film.

In moving waters, trout are most likely to take an imitation ant or beetle presented in a dead drift close to shore or within a backwater, pool, slick, or eddy.

Pattern Notes:
A minuscule (size #28 to #20) dry-fly ant, particularly one that's brightly cinnamon-colored, can raise trout when no other pattern will. Although natural beetles vary in body coloration, most have dark undersides.

Worms, Caterpillars, and Moth Larvae
Aquatic beetles and a variety of waterbugs inhabit moving and still waters of the Front Range. However, their imitations don't hold as much attraction for trout as do patterns that represent other, apparently more appealing foods, such as worms.

During runoff and high-water periods (following a rainfall, for example), earthworms are often washed into ponds and streams. Aquatic worms, which spend their entire lives subsurface, are common year-round. So are aquatic moth larvae. The typical aquatic moth larva is similar in appearance to a caterpillar: wormlike, plump, and encircled with spiky hairs. Like a caterpillar, the larva has six primary legs as well as ten or so leg-like appendages that extend along much of its underside. From June through September, inchworms and caterpillars frequently fall into the water and stimulate feeding among trout.

Patterns: Aquatic worms and earthworms: San Juan Worm. Aquatic moth larvae, inchworms, and caterpillars: Woolly Worm.

Presentations:
Present a San Juan Worm or Woolly Worm in a dead drift, either upstream or down.

Pattern Notes:
The most popular color for a San Juan Worm is pink, brown, or maroon. Though usually tied with a dark chenille body, a bright green, orange, or yellow Woolly Worm can bring the best results. Adult moth imitations are best reserved for nighttime fly fishing (the subject of Jim Bashline's book *Night Fishing for Trout*).

Mosquitoes and Craneflies
Patterns and Presentations:
Because mosquitoes usually inhabit stagnant waters, trout rarely feed on them. If necessary, you can match their larval and

pupal forms with corresponding midge patterns; an Adams or Cahill makes an adequate imitation of an adult mosquito.

Compared to a mosquito, a cranefly is about five times larger. Otherwise, the insects bear a strong resemblance to each other, though craneflies are harmless to humans. Adult craneflies occur near Front Range waters from May through September, but throughout the year trout prefer to feed on the insects' larvae. A cranefly larva's tubular body is similar in appearance to that of a midge larva, but it may grow to a length of nearly 4 inches. The larva is typically a light shade of tan or olive.

The larvae of aquatic craneflies live several inches beneath a streambed—usually, one formed of sand, silt, or gravel. High or otherwise disturbed water flows dislodge the larvae from their sub-streambed homes. These water conditions might occur as a result of runoff, rainfall, flood, dam releases, or animal activity (such as a herd of elk or deer crossing a stream). No matter how high and discolored the water, the presence of drifting cranefly larvae causes voracious feeding among trout. It's usually best to fish the artificial fly with a fair bit of weight clinched onto the tippet; either a down-and-across or up-and-across presentation can be productive. When the time is right, a Cranefly Larva may catch more and bigger trout than any other fly.

Damselflies

Active from June through mid-September, damselflies are chiefly residents of ponds and lakes. Regionally, damselflies are more consequential trout foods than dragonflies, although at first glance the adults of the two insects may appear alike. However, when not in flight, a dragonfly holds its wings out from its sides. In contrast, a resting damselfly holds its wings above and roughly parallel to its body. Damselflies are often referred to simply as damsels, or because of their markedly slender bodies, as flying needles.

Patterns and Presentations:
A typical Front Range damselfly nymph is olive or tan and measures from 15 to 25 mm in length. It's best imitated by a Marabou Damsel Nymph. Large numbers of damselfly nymphs periodically migrate toward shore to emerge, and trout become

keenly interested in feeding on them. A nymph swims for about 8 inches, rests a few seconds, then resumes swimming and resting until it reaches its destination. In pursuit of the preemergent insects, trout often move recklessly close to the shoreline.

The adult damselfly is slightly larger than the nymph. Like mayflies and some caddisflies, a damselfly becomes spent after it has mated and laid eggs. Spent damsels scattered across a pond stimulate trout to surface feed. A Spent Damsel pattern typically features an extended body (made of twisted yarn fibers) and a small, fur thorax wound with a parachute hackle; winging is optional. The fly is best presented to trout already rising to the natural insects.

Scuds, Snails, and Crayfish

Patterns and Presentations:
Scuds, which look like tiny shrimp, live in a variety of Front Range waters, including rivers and ponds, where they can provide a rich food source to trout. Active swimmers, scuds are between 5 and 18 mm long (hook sizes #22 to #10), and their imitations are generally tan, gray, brown, or dull orange in color. Scuds are the most numerous and consequential of Front Range crustaceans, but snails are fairly common too. Snails measuring about 8 to 14 mm in diameter often drift or float within ponds or slow-moving sections of rivers. Trout readily and fiercely consume them. A favorite snail pattern, the Trophy Brown, features a rounded body made of peacock herl. It's simple and it works. Crayfish (or crawdads) resemble small lobsters, and in moving waters, regularly attain a length of about 2 inches. Their imitations are tied on extra-long hooks in sizes #8, #6, and #4. (In large, still waters, crayfish may grow to be more than 7 inches long.) Crayfish are principally creatures of warm-water lakes and so are not as common to the region as scuds and snails. However, sections of some local rivers (notably, the South Platte River from Elevenmile Reservoir upstream to Cheesman Reservoir) support fair populations of them. Look for crayfish in silted stretches of rivers and streams, especially those that flow from or into nearby lakes, ponds, or reservoirs. An imitation of a crayfish, snail, or scud is best presented in a dead-drift occasionally disrupted by subtle, small motions of the rod or line.

Frogs, Mice, Minnows, and Eggs

Patterns and Presentations:

In midsummer and early autumn, during twilight and the hours leading to darkness, an unlucky frog or careless mouse often ends up as a big trout's evening meal. Though ordinarily considered bass-bug patterns, deerhair mice and frog poppers (sizes #8 to #4) work well as trout flies too. A mouse- or frog-fly should be fished similarly to an imitation grasshopper, alternately being twitched and then held motionless on the water. Present the fly in slow-moving or still waters, next to the shore.

Whatever the season, water condition, or time of day, a well-presented streamer can be the most productive of trout flies. Streamers are usually fished as imitations of minnows or other small fish, or as a general-purpose attractor fly. The best patterns include the Gray Ghost, Muddler Minnow, Little Brook Trout, and Woolly Bugger, sizes #14 to #4. The most common streamer presentation involves casting the fly down and across moving currents.

Tied on a curved, short-shank hook in sizes #16 to #10, the spherical, yarn-bodied Glo-Bug represents a fish egg. Bright orange or chartreuse in color, a Glo-Bug is best fished weighted in a dead drift, close to the stream bottom.

Chapter IV
FRONT RANGE FLY-FISHING DESTINATIONS: TRAVEL NOTES

Objects which are usually the motives of our travels
by land and by sea are often overlooked and neglected
if they lie under our eye.

—Pliny the Younger, *Letters*

THE NEXT FIVE chapters describe fifty-seven of the best Front Range fly-fishing destinations, most of which are less than a 90-minute drive from the nearest city. Some fishing sites are roadside, but most require hiking; the hikes generally last less than an hour. Despite their proximity to urban areas, many of the destinations are in wild or sparsely populated places with limited or no services. Before leaving on a trip, make sure your vehicle is in good working order and its gas tank filled. Check the spare tire and jack too. In case of severe weather or other problems, you should always be prepared to spend a night in your car or truck. Carry extra clothing, food, water, and blankets. It's also prudent to have equipment such as flares, a first-aid kit, flashlight, tools, and jumper cables on hand. A dashboard-mounted compass can be convenient when traveling back roads. While driving anywhere near forest or open lands, keep an eye out for deer, elk, and other wildlife. An "Open Range" sign indicates that livestock (including cattle and horses) may be grazing and wandering freely near or on the road.

To find out about road conditions or closures, contact the Colorado Department of Transportation at (303) 639-1111. For stream-flow reports, call Water Talk, a service of the Colorado Division of Water Resources: (303) 831-7135. Both agencies maintain 24-hour-a-day automated telephone services. Front Range fly shops can give you the latest regional fly-fishing news. For additional information, contacts, and phone numbers, refer to the appendix.

AREA MAPS

The *Colorado Atlas and Gazetteer,* published by DeLorme Mapping, contains the road maps referenced here. In Colorado, odd-numbered roads run generally north and south; even-numbered roads, east and west. This convention applies to interstate, U.S., and state highways as well as to county roads. However, in mountainous terrain a road often leads in directions not indicated by its assigned number. For example, most of Colorado 72 lies in the plains, where it follows an east-west course; in the mountains, the road heads north and south. Trails Illustrated and the United States Geological Survey (USGS) produce the most reliable topographic maps. Though U.S. Forest Service maps are helpful for locating trails, roads, and landmarks within a national forest, they are not intended for backcountry use. Offices of the Colorado Division of Wildlife offer maps of state wildlife areas.

LAND MANAGEMENT

Every fly-fishing destination described here is situated on public land—*but private property may be nearby.* Colorado law treats trespassing on private lands as a crime, even where no warning signs are posted. It's your responsibility to know private property boundaries. In addition, most privately held riverfront lands in Colorado have property lines that extend at least to the center point of the streambed. Therefore, you usually can't circumvent boundaries by wading. If you have doubts as to whether a property is public or private, find out before you fish there. Inquire in city, town, or county offices, at the sheriff's department, or at a national forest or national park headquarters. Never walk, wade, or fish on private property unless you have the owner's permission.

The principal Front Range public land management agencies include the Colorado Division of Wildlife, U.S. Forest Service, and National Park Service. The Colorado Division of Wildlife (CDOW) oversees all public fishing waters in the state, including those in the CDOW state wildlife areas. These vary in size from a few hundred to several thousand acres. Many are within national forests; others adjoin private lands. No fees are charged for entrance into a state wildlife area. Regulations are posted at most area entrances. Camping is permitted in some but not all CDOW state wildlife areas. The U.S. Forest Service

(USFS) serves as administrator of the three Front Range national forests: Roosevelt, Arapaho, and Pike. Within national forest boundaries, you'll often find designated USFS recreation areas and wilderness areas. Recreation areas usually feature paved roads, parking lots, rest rooms, and other facilities. Wilderness areas offer few, if any, modern conveniences. The USFS typically posts signs that advise visitors of area regulations. Rules regarding camping, hiking, vehicle use, and other activities may differ from one section of national forest to the next. Depending on the region and time of year, you may have to pay varying fees to enter, park, or camp in a national forest. The National Park Service supervises Rocky Mountain National Park; detailed fishing regulations are available at park visitor centers. Some Front Range county and city governments control their own parks and open spaces, a few of which offer excellent fly fishing. Regulations are generally displayed at entrance areas and trailheads. Front Range lands under the jurisdiction of Colorado State Parks and the Bureau of Land Management (BLM) present limited trout fishing opportunities.

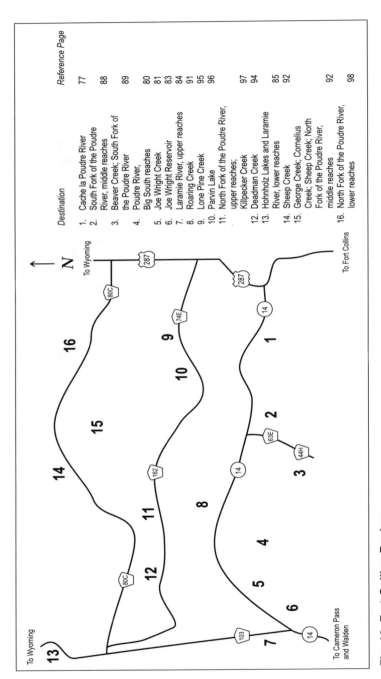

	Reference Page
Destination	
1. Cache la Poudre River	77
2. South Fork of the Poudre River, middle reaches	88
3. Beaver Creek; South Fork of the Poudre River	89
4. Poudre River, Big South reaches	80
5. Joe Wright Creek	81
6. Joe Wright Reservoir	83
7. Laramie River, upper reaches	84
8. Roaring Creek	91
9. Lone Pine Creek	95
10. Parvin Lake	96
11. North Fork of the Poudre River, upper reaches; Killpecker Creek	97
12. Deadman Creek	94
13. Hohnholz Lakes and Laramie River, lower reaches	85
14. Sheep Creek	92
15. George Creek; Cornelius Creek; Sheep Creek; North Fork of the Poudre River, middle reaches	92
16. North Fork of the Poudre River, lower reaches	98

Fig. 13. Fort Collins Region

Chapter V
FORT COLLINS REGION

TODAY FORT COLLINS is a city of more than 90,000 people, home to Colorado State University and high-tech industries. However, traces of an old-west heritage endure. Near the city, U.S. 287 follows a route established by the Overland Trail, the historic stagecoach passage of the middle 1800s. The lands that spread west of the highway probably look much the same now as they did more than a century ago. Most are within Roosevelt National Forest, where the Cache la Poudre River and its tributaries flow. *Cache la poudre* translates from French as "hide the powder." Legend holds that a group of Hudson Bay traders in the 1830s faced a snowstorm while traveling in what is now known as the Cache la Poudre Canyon. One of the traders stated they should unload and conceal their heavy store of gunpowder. "*Cache la poudre,*" he supposedly said, and so the river and canyon were named. Other site names around the Poudre don't require translation, but they still resonate with the toughness of pioneer America. You might fish Deadman Creek, which is in Deadman Park, off Deadman Road. En route, you may travel near Horsethief Pass, Poverty Flats, and Killpecker Creek.

Once you head north and west of Fort Collins, past Laporte and Teds Place, you won't see another town for miles. Though there are several small settlements in and around the Poudre Canyon, just a few have shops or restaurants; fewer still have gas stations. The homes scattered through the area belong mostly to cattle ranchers or summer residents. A maze of gulches and ravines cuts through the surrounding foothills and mountains. It's an easy place to get lost (or at least disoriented), especially when you leave the main roads. Several years ago, I was fishing a tiny creek north of the Poudre River when a man about seventy years old approached me. The creek was accessible only by a nameless, dead-end jeep trail. He asked how to get back to the highway. With a little smile, he said, "It's not that I'm lost, you understand. I just don't know where I'm at." Many of the old back roads around Poudre Canyon are unmapped, risky, and lead nowhere. If a backcountry road isn't indicated by a USFS or CDOW sign or map, avoid driving on it. Otherwise, even if you don't get lost, you probably won't know where you're at. Watch out for rattlers at elevations below 7,000 feet; some canyons create a fine habitat for them. When driving or hiking in a canyon, look out for rock slides too. They often occur during or soon after a rainfall, or as ice freezes or thaws on the mountainsides. Of course, there's more to the Poudre Canyon area than bad roads, rattlers, and rock slides. Probably no other place along the Front Range holds as many different and beautiful places to fish.

CACHE LA POUDRE RIVER ALONG COLORADO 14
(See map page 76.)

Management: USFS; CDOW; private.

Area maps: USFS map, Roosevelt and Arapaho national forests; Trails Illustrated maps 101 and 112; DeLorme maps 20, 19, and 18.

Elevations: From 5,700 to 8,500 feet.

Hiking distance: Most destinations are roadside. However, reaching the river near Indian Meadows may require up to a 0.25-mile walk.

Hike rating: Easy.

Special regulations: In two areas, fishing is restricted to artificial flies or lures, and the trout bag and possession limit is two fish 16 inches or longer. The areas extend (1) from the Pingree Park Road (County Road 63E) bridge upstream to Rustic and (2) from Black Hollow Creek (near Idylwilde) upstream to the Big Bend Campground (which lies east of Kinikinik and west of the fish hatchery).

Directions: From Fort Collins, take U.S. 287 north to Colorado 14 west, which follows the river for about 46 miles.

More than 40 miles of the Cache la Poudre River flow alongside Colorado 14 through the rugged Cache la Poudre Canyon. The river (commonly called "the Poudre") has no dams, but diversion structures reroute some of its water for agricultural and municipal use. On some days, water levels may vary noticeably, although the changes rarely have a negative effect on fishing conditions. During runoff season, the river is popular with whitewater rafters and kayakers. The number of boaters decreases as the water drops to levels better suited to fishing. The river and canyon often become crowded on summer weekends, too, when tourists and locals come to picnic, sightsee, hike, camp, and fish. The river fishes best from early April through mid-June, and from late July through mid-November. During the summer and early autumn, make your trips there on weekdays to avoid any crowds. An 8- to 9-foot-long, 4-weight rod can handle most Poudre fly fishing, and wading the river is generally easy. Forest Service signs clearly identify the canyon's many campgrounds and other riverside facilities.

Landmark	Distance from junction of U.S. 287 and Colorado 14	Elevation (feet)
Diamond Rock Picnic Ground	11.2 miles	5,760
Indian Meadows Campground	27.1 miles	6,900
State Fish Hatchery	37.3 miles	7,700
Big South Trailhead	46.7 miles	8,500

The prime fishing lies west of the Diamond Rock Picnic Ground. From Diamond Rock upstream to the Big South Trailhead, most of the river moves quickly over a gently sloping, rocky streambed. Averaging 30 to 60 feet wide, the Poudre flows alternately in runs, pools, pockets, glides, and riffles. Occasionally the river channel narrows, creating chutes and plunge pools. Fast-water sections of the Poudre hold large populations of net-spinning caddisflies. The Caddis Larva (either green or dark olive, sizes #16 to #10) rates among the most productive subsurface flies. So do the C.Q. Gordon and Hare's Ear, sizes #16 to #12. When fishing dry flies, concentrate your presentations near the shorelines—some of the river's best and least-fished areas. From summer to early fall, there are good hatches of quill gordon and red quill mayflies (sizes #16 to #12). Green drakes emerge occasionally as well. When trout aren't rising, try presenting a small (sizes #22 to #20) parachute Adams or Gray Midge in the slack waters next to the bank.

The river slows its pace in the flatlands around Indian Meadows and the state fish hatchery. Especially near the hatchery, the meandering, silt-bottomed waters seem as delicate and spooky as a spring creek. In both places, a long (up to 14-foot) leader tapered to 6X can help you fool some sizable trout. Watch for hatches and spinner falls of pale morning duns, blue-winged olives, and tricos. Midges (sizes #24 to #14) are common too. When adult caddisflies begin skittering on fast- or slow-moving waters, remember that a down-and-across presentation of a soft-hackle fly (such as a Partridge-and-Orange) is still one of the best fly-fishing techniques around. The Poudre's trout include browns, rainbows, and cutts that ordinarily range from 10 to 16 inches long. Rocky Mountain whitefish also live in the river, mainly in the stretch between Stove Prairie Landing and Dutch George Flats.

CACHE LA POUDRE RIVER, BIG SOUTH REACHES
(See map page 76.)

Management: USFS; National Park Service.

Area maps: USFS map, Roosevelt and Arapaho national forests; Trails Illustrated map 112; DeLorme maps 20, 19, and 18.

Elevations: Trailhead: 8,440 feet. Destination: About 8,600 feet.

Hiking distance: 0.5 mile.

Hike rating: Easy to moderate.

Special regulations: From the river's confluence with Joe Wright Creek upstream to Rocky Mountain National Park, fishing is restricted to artificial flies or lures. The bag and possession limit is two fish.

Directions: From Fort Collins, take U.S. 287 north to Colorado 14 west. Follow Colorado 14 about 46.7 miles and turn left (south and east) at the Big South Trailhead parking area, located about 1 mile south of Poudre Falls. Hike the Big South Trail (#944) along the Cache la Poudre River.

Near the Big South Trailhead and Campground, the Poudre moves out of the view of motorists on Colorado 14. (The water that continues to parallel the road for several miles is Joe Wright Creek, discussed later.) The Big South Trail winds south and west, tracing the Poudre's course for about 20 miles to the river's headwaters in Rocky Mountain National Park. Along the way, the trail merges with the Cache la Poudre Trail. However, you won't need to travel such a long distance to appreciate the special character and wonderful fishing of the Poudre's upper reaches. Hike the trail for only about a half mile and you'll enter the Comanche Peak Wilderness Area of Roosevelt National Forest.

There the Poudre resembles a mountain stream, racing through narrow canyons and over a steep, boulder-strewn streambed. Seldom more than about 25 feet wide, the river provides superb habitat to brown, brook, rainbow, and cutthroat trout, most between 9 and 11 inches long. Be careful wading in this area, especially in times of high water, because the rocky stream bottom is extremely uneven. There's great pocket-water fishing in the plunge pools, chutes, and riffles. Occasional deep pools and runs accommodate longer-line presentations and also hold some of the larger trout. An 8-foot rod is the longest you will need.

The streamside trail moves through stands of lodgepole and aspen, and over the tops of canyon walls. From vantage points on the trail, you'll often have a good view into the exceptionally clear water. Because of the surrounding canyons and trees, the river receives only limited exposure to sunlight. As a result, the water temperature usually measures at least a few degrees cooler than it does in the Poudre's roadside stretches. The major aquatic insects include green sedges, golden stoneflies, quill gordons, and red quills. The Prince Stonefly Nymph (sizes #10 to #8), Caddis Larva (green, sizes #16 to #10), and C.Q. Gordon (sizes #14 to #12) are among the most productive subsurface patterns. For a dry fly, try a Royal Wulff, Deerhair Caddis, or Red Quill in sizes #16 to #12.

JOE WRIGHT CREEK
(See map page 76.)

Management: USFS.

Area maps: USFS map, Roosevelt and Arapaho national forests; Trails Illustrated map 112; DeLorme maps 20, 19, and 18.

Average elevation: About 8,700 feet.

Hiking distance: Roadside. Reaching some sections of the creek may require walking up to 0.25 mile.

Hike rating: Easy.

Special regulations: From Joe Wright Reservoir upstream to Colorado 14, fishing is restricted to artificial flies or lures. The bag and possession limit is two trout of 16 inches or longer. The creek in that area is closed to fishing from January 1 to July 31.

Directions: From Fort Collins, take U.S. 287 north to Colorado 14 west. Follow Colorado 14 about 46.7 miles and turn left (south and east) at the Big South Trailhead parking area, located about 1 mile south of Poudre Falls. The confluence of Joe Wright Creek and the Cache la Poudre River is a few hundred yards downstream of the parking area. Joe Wright Creek flows along or near Colorado 14 as the road heads south and west from Big South toward Cameron Pass.

The best stretch of Joe Wright Creek flows between the creek's confluence with the Poudre River and the outlet of Joe Wright Reservoir. Though the streambanks are steep, it's easiest to walk along the southern shoreline where willows and evergreens grow. Scree (an unstable layer of loose, broken rock) covers much of the mountainside that forms the creek's north bank.

The creek measures from 20 to 30 feet wide and runs at a fairly rapid pace. Trout (mainly browns) hold near the boulders and other large rocks that line the streambed. Most of the creek flows in pocket waters interspersed with small, deep pools. Plan on fishing a short line. Unless there's a hatch or other insect activity to stimulate surface feeding, the trout usually keep close to the stream bottom. However, you might raise a fish with a well-placed terrestrial pattern; large numbers of grasshoppers and black ants live on the shore. From mid-July to late August, the creek produces fair emergences of little green stoneflies, yellow sallies, and red quills. Green sedges also thrive in the fast, rocky waters. Stock up on the Henryville Special, Caddis Larva, and Grizzly-and-Orange, sizes #16 to #12.

JOE WRIGHT RESERVOIR
(See map page 76.)

Management: USFS; CDOW.

Area maps: USFS map, Roosevelt and Arapaho national forests; Trails Illustrated map 112; DeLorme maps 20, 19, and 18.

Average elevation: About 10,000 feet.

Hiking distance: 0.25 mile.

Hike rating: Easy.

Special regulations: Fishing is restricted to artificial flies or lures. The trout bag and possession limit is two fish of 16 inches or longer.

Directions: From Fort Collins, take U.S. 287 north to Colorado 14 west. Follow Colorado 14 about 54.8 miles and turn left (south and east) at the Joe Wright Reservoir parking lot. Joe Wright Reservoir and Joe Wright Creek are visible from the parking lot. Both sides of the creek have well-worn but un-marked trails that lead to the reservoir. Hike one of the trails north (downstream) about 0.25 mile.

The fish you'll most often see rising near the reservoir's shores aren't trout but grayling. Like its close relative, the Rocky Mountain whitefish, a grayling has a tiny mouth, forked tail, and pronounced scales. However, a grayling's dorsal (top) fin is iridescent and disproportionately large. When fly fishing for grayling, use flies tied on hook sizes #16 and smaller. Larger hooks seldom hold. You'll also need to slow the timing and re-duce the power of your hook-sets. Grayling not only have small, soft-tissued mouths, they often strike repeatedly at a fly before seizing it. For what it's worth: Weighted, green-and-yel-low subsurface flies (such as a Tellico Nymph, Woolly Worm, or Emergent Sparkle Pupa) probably catch more grayling than any other pattern. No one knows why. Apart from these few exceptions, fly fishing for grayling is pretty much like fly fish-ing for trout. Grayling can be just as fussy and unpredictable, and they're great fun to catch.

The grayling in Joe Wright Reservoir (which covers about 160 acres) average about 9 to 13 inches long. Look for the best fishing within 500 yards or so of the reservoir's in-let (southern) end. Float tubes and non-motorized boats are allowed, but you don't need one to enjoy the area. Fishing near or from the shore is worthwhile and easier. Be careful along the eastern banks; they're slippery and steep. The reservoir also holds some Emerald Lake rainbows, a brightly colored trout species introduced to the Front Range from southwestern Colorado. For most fly anglers, though, it's difficult to concentrate on trout when exotic, elusive grayling are around.

If you'd like to pursue fly fishing for grayling, check out nearby Zimmerman Lake. The Zimmerman Lake Trailhead is just a few hundred yards south and west of the Joe Wright Reservoir inlet. Hike the Zimmerman Lake Trail (# 941) about 1.7 miles to the lake. See if you can top Zimmerman's state-record grayling of 1974: a 15-inch fish that weighed 23 ounces. A small green-and-yellow nymph should do the job. Then you can return to the serious business of fly fishing for trout.

LARAMIE RIVER, UPPER REACHES
(See map page 76.)

Management: USFS; private.

Area maps: USFS map, Roosevelt and Arapaho national forests; Trails Illustrated map 112; DeLorme maps 20, 19, and 18.

Average elevation: 8,550 feet.

Hiking distance: Most of the river is roadside; however, reaching some sections of the Laramie may require up to a 0.3-mile walk.

Hike rating: Easy.

Special regulations: None. (Special regulations apply only to the stretch of the Laramie River that flows in the Hohnholz State Wildlife Area.)

Directions: From Fort Collins, take U.S. 287 north to Colorado 14 west. Follow Colorado 14 about 49.3 miles and turn right (north) on County Road 103, located around 2.6 miles south and west of the Big South Trailhead parking area. Continue about 2.7 miles north, passing Chambers Lake on the left (east) side of the road. County Road 103 runs adjacent to public waters of the upper Laramie River for about 8.5 miles to the north. The river moves generally south-to-north as it flows from Colorado downstream to Wyoming.

Mostly browns and brookies populate this reach of the Laramie. The river is small, averaging only about 15 to 20 feet wide. It flows along a gentle gradient through sage-filled meadows and groves of evergreen and aspen. In the river's exposed meadow stretches, water moves in riffles and glides. Trout there are skittish. You'll need to keep a low profile and cast a light line, especially when fishing dry flies. Small (sizes #20 to #16) Comparaduns and Parachute Blue-Winged Olives are especially productive. Where the streambed narrows and trees overhang the banks, the river runs more quickly. In these places, short-line presentations of a heavily weighted nymph (such as a Hare's Ear or Pheasant Tail, sizes #20 to #16) work best. Take time to explore the Laramie's side waters and feeder creeks (including the west branch of the Laramie River, near the Tunnel Campground). The largest trout often hold in or near them. Watch for beaver ponds too; they're scattered along both sides of the river. Local old-timers say that beavers have lived around the upper Laramie River for at least the past sixty years. It's difficult to predict the exact location or condition of beaver lodges, dams, and ponds from one year to the next. For example, flooding and runoff often breach beaver dams. Beavers generally renovate or replace a dam that's been weakened or destroyed. However, they might rebuild on the original site or construct a new dam somewhere else. Wherever you find them, beaver ponds near the Laramie teem with midges, most of them olive-gray, sizes #24 to #18. Most of the ponds hold brown and brook trout from 8 to 11 inches long. The Laramie's public waters end near the Rawah Trailhead and Rawah Guest Ranch, about 5 miles north of the Tunnel Campground. Roughly 15.5 miles north of the Rawah Trailhead, another stretch of the river opens to the public in the Hohnholz State Wildlife Area.

LARAMIE RIVER (LOWER REACHES) AND THE HOHNHOLZ LAKES
(See map page 76.)

Management: USFS; CDOW; BLM; private.

Area maps: USFS map, Roosevelt and Arapaho national forests; Trails Illustrated maps 111 and 113; DeLorme maps 20, 19, and 18.

Average elevation: About 7,900 feet.

Hiking distance: Most fishing areas are within 100 yards of a road or parking area.

Hike rating: Easy.

Special regulations: Laramie River: Fishing is restricted to artificial flies or lures, and the trout bag and possession limit is two fish.

Hohnholz Lakes: Fishing in Hohnholz Lake #3 is restricted to artificial flies or lures, and the trout bag and possession limit is four fish.

Directions: To the lower Laramie River: From Fort Collins, take U.S. 287 north to Colorado 14 west. Follow Colorado 14 about 49.3 miles and turn right (north) on County Road 103, located around 2.6 miles south and west of the Big South Trailhead parking area. Drive on County Road 103 for a total of around 26.7 miles. After traveling about 14.9 miles, you'll come to a fork in the road. At that point, be sure to turn right (east) in order to stay on County Road 103, which soon resumes a northerly course. Turn left (west and south) on Forest Road 200, which is marked by a state wildlife area sign. Continue another 0.5 mile to a parking area and a bridge across the Laramie River.

To the Hohnholz Lakes: From the Laramie River bridge, follow Forest Road 200 about 0.9 mile to Hohnholz Lake #1; 1.7 miles to Lake #2; and 3.3 miles to Lake #3.

Note: The drive from Fort Collins to the Hohnholz State Wildlife Area takes about 2.5 hours—by far the longest road trip described in this book.

Laramie River

This stretch of river is just a mile long, with fishing allowed 0.5 mile upstream and downstream of the bridge. To comply with easement rules and to avoid trespassing on adjacent private land, you'll need to keep within 20 feet of the high-water line. In its lower reaches, the Laramie is about 25 feet wide and moves across a rocky, algae-coated streambed. Willows and aspen along the banks help shelter the river from wind. The trout (mostly browns, brookies, and a few rainbows) hold in the river's many undercut banks, pockets, and riffles. Other sections of the Laramie flow in broad, shallow glides, some more than 50 feet long. The best dry-fly patterns for the Laramie are low-floating and sparsely dressed: the Henryville Special (without palmered hackle), Spent Partridge Caddis, Comparadun, Parachute Adams, and Parachute Emerger. Pale morning duns and blue-winged olives are among the river's most common mayflies, but caddisflies outnumber them. Watch for the American grannom, the tan short-horn sedge, and about a half-dozen other kinds of caddis. Subsurface patterns such as the Latex Larva, Herl Nymph, and Prince Nymph all perform well. In the river's riffles and glides, try presenting any of them down- and across-stream.

The Hohnholz Lakes

Eight-acre Lake #1 (shown on some maps as East Lake) offers limited fishing opportunities; by summer's end, the lake is often dry. Lakes #2 and #3 cover about 35 and 42 acres, respectively. Fishing these larger lakes can be wonderful, though a bit perplexing at first. Each is a nearly featureless basin, outlined only by the grass and sage of the surrounding high prairie. No trees grow along the banks; no rocks rise from the water. No inlets or promontories alter the shape of the shoreline. Regardless, both lakes hold large numbers of rainbows, cutts, and browns, many up to 3 pounds or more. But where to fish?

Fishing in Lake #2 (also known as Little Hohnholz) is generally best around the lake's southern end. In Lake #3, it's most fun and productive to fish from a float tube. Start by checking out the waters near the southern and eastern shores. Keep in mind, though, that trout might be cruising or holding nearly anywhere in the lake, sections of which measure more than 30 feet deep. A sinking-tip line comes in handy there. In the exposed terrain around the lakes, winds often blow at sustained speeds of 30 mph or more. When winds blow across most still waters, trout typically migrate toward the leeward shores. In the Hohnholz Lakes, however, trout usually respond to windy conditions by moving to greater depths. The Renegade and Black Gnat (sizes #22 to #18) rate as two of the best dry-fly patterns. Time-tested, they've been fooling Hohnholz trout for over forty years. Tan scuds (sizes #14 to #18) and dark, leech-type flies (such as Zonkers and Woolly Buggers) work well subsurface.

One of the more intriguing events on Lake #3 occurs from middle to late summer. Around dusk and soon after, brown trout move into the shallows to feed. Mice and other small rodents become active about the same time; large browns eat them when they can. Using a stout-butted, 8-foot leader tapered to 3X, present a deer-hair mouse (its body length between 0.5 and 1.25 inches) tight against the shore. Every ten seconds or so, twitch the mouse-fly slightly, moving it just a fraction of an inch. Let the fly rest for another several seconds before you move it again. In the dim light, you probably won't see a large brown striking the fly, but you'll almost certainly hear it. Then set the hook and keep a tight line. By the time you get back to Fort Collins, at least a couple of the microbreweries might still be open.

SOUTH FORK OF THE CACHE LA POUDRE RIVER, MIDDLE AND UPPER REACHES
(See map page 76.)

Management: USFS; private.

Area maps: USFS map, Roosevelt and Arapaho national forests; Trails Illustrated maps 101 and 112; DeLorme maps 20 and 19.

Average elevation: 8,500 feet.

Hiking distance: Most destinations are roadside. However, reaching some sections of the river may require up to a 0.25-mile walk.

Hike rating: Easy.

Special regulations: None.

Directions: From Fort Collins, take U.S. 287 north to Colorado 14 west. Follow Colorado 14 about 25.3 miles and turn left (south) on County Road 63E (Pingree Park Road), located about 1.2 miles west of the Kelly Flats Campground.

Middle reaches of the South Fork: Follow County Road 63E about 7.5 miles. The river flows near the road.

Upper reaches of the South Fork: Follow County Road 63E about 11.4 miles, at which point County Road 63E merges with County Road 44H. Follow County Road 44H south and west about 3.4 miles and turn right (north) on Forest Road 145 to the Tom Bennett Campground, a few hundred yards from the county road. The river runs through the campground.

You'll first see the South Fork on the east (left) side of County Road 63E. These middle reaches run mostly in pockets and riffles across a cobbled streambed. From 20 to 30 feet

wide, the river cuts through about 4 miles of meadow bordered by spruce and aspen. As you head farther upstream (toward Tom Bennett Campground) the land surrounding the
South Fork becomes more heavily forested. Upper reaches of
the river move along a faster, more narrow gradient. Several
miles of water remain open to public fishing, but some sections
are on private property. Near the Lazy D Ranch and the confluence of Pennock Creek, the South Fork drops from view as
it turns east and south. A lovely 2-mile stretch of the river
flows from Tom Bennett Campground downstream to the confluence of Beaver Creek. Upstream of the campground, the
river again crosses private land. The South Fork's highest regions are accessible only by long, challenging, difficult backcountry trails.

You might want to explore the South Fork where it joins
the Poudre. The confluence lies on the Poudre's south side,
about 700 yards west (upstream) from the Century Park Picnic
Ground on Colorado 14. However, the trip has drawbacks.
Crossing the Poudre in that area might be tricky, especially
when flows are high. Just finding the confluence can be a challenge too. Its location is masked by clefts in the canyon walls
and islands in the main river. If you do make it into the lowest
reaches of the South Fork, be cautious when walking the
shores. Rattlers are probably nearby.

South Fork trout include browns, brookies, rainbows,
cutts, and cuttbows that generally range from 8 to 12 inches
long. Large numbers of golden stonefly nymphs and American
grannom larvae live on the streambed. Grasshoppers frequent
the banks, especially in meadows and other areas exposed to
south light. Two-fly rigs work well in much of the river. For example, try using a size #14 Stimulator or size #10 Parachute
Hopper as a point fly. About 18 to 24 inches below it, tie on a
size #16 Herl Nymph or Prince Nymph. On a good day, you
may need nothing more.

BEAVER CREEK
(See map page 76.)

Management: USFS; private.

Area maps: USFS map, Roosevelt and Arapaho national forests;
Trails Illustrated maps 101 and 112; DeLorme maps 20 and 19.

Average elevation: About 9,000 feet.

Hiking distance: From 0.1 mile to 2 miles.

Hike rating: Easy to moderate.

Special regulations: None.

Directions: From Fort Collins, take U.S. 287 north to Colorado 14 west. Follow Colorado 14 about 25.3 miles and turn left (south) onto County Road 63E (Pingree Park Road), located about 1.2 miles west of the Kelly Flats Campground. Follow County Road 63E about 11.4 miles, at which point County Road 63E merges with County Road 44H. Follow County Road 44H south and west about 3.4 miles and turn right (north) on Forest Road 145 to the Tom Bennett Campground, a few hundred yards from the county road. From the campground, follow Forest Road 145 north and west (toward the Cirque Meadow Trailhead and the Fish Creek and Beaver Creek trailheads) about 0.9 mile. The road crosses the creek; parking areas are nearby.

Downstream (east) of the road, Beaver Creek is fast, steep, and narrow, its banks filled with willows and pines. Unmarked trails follow the creek on its 2-mile run down to the South Fork of the Poudre. On this stretch, short-line presentations are most productive. The fish aren't big, only about 8 to 10 inches long. However, like many other small mountain brooks, Beaver Creek has high concentrations of pale western stream sedges, some of the largest caddisflies found in the Front Range. In late summer and early autumn, a size #10 Colorado King is especially effective. Don't be disappointed if you have trouble hooking some of the trout that rise to the fly. Chances are, they're just too small to get hold of it. Sometimes, even on a little creek, fishing a big dry fly means you'll catch only the biggest trout.

Upstream (west) of the road, the water broadens and flows through terrain that's more level. After about 500 yards, though, the creek crosses private property, where trespassing is prohibited. The Beaver Creek Trailhead lies a few hundred yards west and north of where Forest Road 145 crosses the creek. Over a roughly 8-mile course and a 2,000-foot elevation gain, the Beaver Creek Trail (#942) parallels the creek to its headwaters in the Mummy Range. Lots of folks have traveled that entire route, but I'm not one of them. I've hiked only about 2 miles west and south of the trailhead. Fishing there is fine.

ROARING CREEK
(See map page 76.)

Management: USFS.

Area maps: USFS map, Roosevelt and Arapaho national forests; Trails Illustrated map 112; DeLorme maps 20 and 19.

Elevations: Trailhead: 8,000 feet. Destination: 8,700 feet.

Hiking distance: 1.5 miles.

Hike rating: Moderate to slightly difficult.

Special regulations: None.

Directions: From Fort Collins, take U.S. 287 north to Colorado 14 west. Follow Colorado 14 about 38.8 miles and turn right (north) at the Roaring Creek Trailhead parking area, located about 1.5 miles west of the state fish hatchery. Hike the Roaring Creek Trail (sometimes called the Roaring Fork Trail) to Roaring Creek.

The trail ascends sharply during its first mile. Then it enters relatively level terrain, paralleling the creek (which lies nearby to the west) for about another mile. That's where you'll find the best fishing. However, Roaring Creek is a small water that holds small fish. If you love fly fishing in tiny creeks for little trout, make the trip. Otherwise, don't go there. Most sections of the creek measure no more than 8 feet across. Nearly all its trout are greenback cutts, most just 6 to 8 inches long. In 1997 beavers around Roaring Creek were beginning to rebuild numerous dams destroyed by past flooding and runoff. Within the next several years, there's a good chance that some stretches of the creek may again become dammed and ponded. Maybe the cutts will grow too. Incidentally, Roaring Creek greenbacks are not considered "genetically pure," therefore no special fishing regulations protect them.

SHEEP CREEK, GEORGE CREEK, CORNELIUS CREEK, AND THE NORTH FORK OF THE CACHE LA POUDRE RIVER, MIDDLE REACHES
(See map page 76.)

Management: CDOW; USFS; private.

Area maps: USFS map, Roosevelt and Arapaho national forests; Trails Illustrated map 111; DeLorme maps 20 and 19.

Average elevation: 7,700 feet.

Hiking distance: Reaching most of these four destinations requires a hike of 1 mile or less.

Hike rating: Easy to moderate.

Special regulations: These waters flow through the Cherokee Park State Wildlife Area, which is closed to the public from March 1 to Memorial Day. On George and Cornelius Creeks, fishing is restricted to catch-and-release with artificial flies or lures. 22.6 past mile marker 22

Directions: From Fort Collins, take U.S. 287 north to County Road 80C west. Drive 21.8 miles on County Road 80C, then turn left (south) on the road marked by a state wildlife area sign. Continue 4 miles to the road's end at the Sheep Creek Campground. The area offers relatively easy access to four trout streams. However, some trails are poorly defined; none are marked. Use a topographic map and compass for reference.

Sheep Creek
Sheep Creek runs adjacent to the campground. You can follow the creek upstream for about 1.6 miles through meadows and woods before the water enters private land. Averaging 10 to 15 feet wide, Sheep Creek flows along a rocky but gentle gradient. Willows and brush overhang much of the water, providing cover for the creek's browns, brookies, and rainbows. Make most of your presentations upstream and close to the banks, many of which are undercut. In summer and autumn, grasshoppers abound in nearby grasses. (So do garter snakes; they're harmless.) Other streamside vegetation often holds a variety of caddisflies, as well as little green stoneflies and yellow sallies. The trout generally range from 9 to 12 inches long. A similar, publicly accessible stretch of Sheep

Creek runs just south of the county road. From U.S. 287, follow County Road 80C 23.7 miles west. At that point, you'll see the creek and a state wildlife area sign. Roadside parking is nearby.

Cornelius Creek and George Creek

Too small [handwritten]

There are two routes to Cornelius Creek. Cross Sheep Creek near the campground and walk about two hundred yards downstream. The first small stream that flows into Sheep Creek from the west is Cornelius Creek. However, wading or hiking upstream along this stretch of Cornelius Creek is slow and difficult. As an alternative, you can hike the old four-wheel-drive road that lies a few hundred yards west of the confluence of Cornelius Creek and Sheep Creek. The route used to be part of Forest Road 313, but today it's closed to vehicles and unmarked by signs. During the first 0.5 mile or so, the road bends north and west, away from the creek. After a few hundred yards, the road again nears the water. Hike another 0.5 mile more and you'll reach the confluence of George Creek (to the north) and Cornelius Creek.

Strictly for the small-stream aficionado, both creeks are narrow (6 to 8 feet across) and brushy. However, they hold strong populations of greenback cutts as well as lesser numbers of brookies, browns, and rainbows. Each stream flows in a fairly straight, deep channel bounded by grassy and deeply undercut banks. The farther upstream you travel along either creek, the more likely you'll begin seeing beaver dams and ponds. You probably won't encounter any other fly anglers, but you may meet a moose or two.

North Fork of the Cache la Poudre River, Middle Reaches

walk in meadows on south side [handwritten]

You can get to the North Fork from the campground area by following Sheep Creek downstream about 0.3 mile. A small footpath lies along part of the creek's north shore, and the creek flows into the river. Downstream of the confluence, the North Fork runs along a nearly level gradient through pastureland and forest. Hiking and wading there are comparatively easy, though you can't rely upon a continuous riverside trail. Upstream of the confluence, the river steepens as it flows through a stony canyon. Terrain there is stunning and wild, and travel

Did well w/ swear bodied Elkhair Caddis 7/22/01 [handwritten]

slow and rough. What may begin as an adequate trail might suddenly end at an impassable cliff or rockslide. When this occurs, you'll have to head back downstream, wade to the opposite bank, and find another path.

Both stretches of the river have a rocky, uneven streambed that averages from 15 to 20 feet wide. Some of the best subsurface flies to use in the middle reaches of the North Fork include the C.Q. Gordon (sizes #14 to #12) and 20-Inch Nymph (sizes #8 to #4). The Comparadun (medium olive, sizes #18 to #16), Red Quill (sizes #16 to #12), and Colorado King (sizes #14 to #8) rate among the most effective dry flies. The trout are mainly browns from 9 to 11 inches long.

DEADMAN CREEK
(See map page 76.)

Management: USFS.

Area maps: USFS map, Roosevelt and Arapaho national forests; Trails Illustrated map 111; DeLorme maps 20, 19, and 18.

Elevation: 9,800 feet.

Hiking distance: The creek flows within a few hundred feet of the road.

Hike rating: Easy.

Special regulations: None.

Directions: From Fort Collins, take U.S. 287 north to County Road 74E west. Follow County Road 74E about 23.3 miles, at which point County Road 74E merges into County Road 162, also known as Deadman Road. Follow County Road 162 west for about 13.4 miles and turn left (south) on Forest Road 319. Drive south and west for 1 mile on Forest Road 319 to the south side of Deadman Creek in Deadman Park.

A little stream filled with small brook trout, Deadman Creek flows through a high mountain plain. Cattle graze on the huge hillsides that rise to the north and west. Parts of the creek run in long, narrow channels; others pour into broad pools. Low-growing grasses and sage line the banks. Tiny pebbles that encrust the streambed rocks are actually the larval cases of the tan short-horn sedge. Cast a Rubber Band Nymph or Partridge-and-Orange down- and across-stream, and you'll probably start catching brookies. Though small, the trout are as wary as they are wild, and they'll scatter at the first hint of danger. Approach the water cautiously and wade as little as you can. It's most fun to fish Deadman Creek with a 2- or 3-weight rod up to nine feet long. Whatever rod you use, rig it with a 9- to 10-foot leader tapered to 5X or finer.

LONE PINE CREEK, LONE PINE STATE WILDLIFE AREA
(See map page 76.)

Management: USFS; CDOW; private.

Area maps: USFS map, Roosevelt and Arapaho national forests; CDOW map, Cherokee Park State Wildlife Area: Lower Lone Pine Units; USGS maps, Livermore Mountain and Haystack Gulch; DeLorme maps 20 and 19.

Average elevation: About 6,300 feet.

Hiking distance: 0.7 mile.

Hike rating: Easy.

Special regulations: This state wildlife area is open to public use from June 15 until the Saturday before the archery hunting season, which usually begins in late August. For more information regarding the hunting seasons, contact the Colorado Division of Wildlife.

Directions: From Fort Collins, take U.S. 287 north to County Road 74E west. Follow County Road 74E about 7.5 miles and turn right (north) into a parking area marked by a state wildlife area sign. From the gate in the northeast side of the parking area, hike east along the dirt road. The road curves to the west and leads to the creek. Follow the creek upstream (west); downstream land is private.

Lone Pine Creek flows through a small but strikingly beautiful high desert valley. Yucca, sage, and flowering cactus grow on the rolling hills that rise north and south of the water. If you intend to fish there, you'll need a great love of little streams and a short fly rod. Many of Lone Pine's lower stretches are only about 8 feet wide. However, especially where the streambed moves close to shoreline rock outcroppings, the water often measures more than 4 feet deep. Push your way through the cottonwood and willow that overhang much of the creek and you'll occasionally find deep pools and glides nearly 20 feet in diameter. Small-stream anglers delight in this sort of thing; everyone else knows we're crazy. The only nearby trail (most often used as a horse trail) is worn but unsigned. It follows the south shore of the creek for about 1 mile to the west, then crosses the water. The trail continues about another 0.8 mile west and north before leaving the state wildlife area and entering Roosevelt National Forest. Most of the trout in Lone Pine Creek are browns from 8 to 12 inches long.

PARVIN LAKE
(See map page 76.)

Management: CDOW.

Area maps: USFS map, Roosevelt and Arapaho national forests; CDOW map, Dowdy, Parvin, West, and Bellaire Lakes state wildlife areas; USGS map, Red Feather Lakes; DeLorme maps 20 and 19.

Elevation: 8,200 feet.

Hiking distance: 0.25 mile.

Hike rating: Easy.

Special regulations: Fishing is restricted to artificial flies or lures. The lake is closed to fishing from November 1 to April 30. From May 1 to October 31, fishing is permitted only between 4 A.M. and 10 P.M. Other rules are posted at the Parvin Lake entrance station.

Directions: From Fort Collins, take U.S. 287 north to County Road 74E west. Follow County Road 74E about 21.1 miles and turn right (north) into a parking area marked by a state wildlife area sign.

Float-tube here if you can. Parvin Lake covers more than 60 acres and reaches depths of 30 feet. The best fishing usually occurs in early morning and around dusk. Midge patterns (sizes #24 to #20) and yellow-olive scuds (sizes #22 to #18) work well throughout the lake, especially near the western shores. Around the deep northern outlet, heavily weighted streamers (such as a size #10 Little Brook Trout or Woolly Bugger) can be effective even at midday. Deadfall and drop-offs lie along much of the lake's rocky east banks, a prime area for shore fishing. Trout there frequently rise to dry-fly ants and other small terrestrials. Since 1949, the Colorado Division of Wildlife has used Parvin Lake as a research model for sport-fishing management. The lake's trout may include cutts, rainbows, and browns.

KILLPECKER CREEK AND THE NORTH FORK OF THE CACHE LA POUDRE RIVER, UPPER REACHES
(See map page 76.)

Management: USFS.

Area maps: USFS map, Roosevelt and Arapaho national forests; Trails Illustrated map 111; DeLorme maps 20 and 19.

Elevation: 9,300 feet.

Hiking distance: 0.5 mile.

Hike rating: Easy.

Special regulations: None.

Directions: From Fort Collins, take U.S. 287 north to County Road 74E west. Follow County Road 74E about 23.3 miles, at which point County Road 74E merges into County Road 162, also known as Deadman Road. Follow County Road 162 west for about 6.6 miles and turn left (south) into the parking area for the Killpecker Creek Trailhead. The Killpecker Trail (#956) follows the creek upstream.

Killpecker Creek

On your way to Killpecker Creek, stop awhile at the North Lone Pine Overlook, located about 4 miles west of the beginning of Deadman Road. The views are as grand as any you'll see in the Front Range. Then drive another 2.6 miles to the Killpecker Trailhead. A hundred yards or so downstream from the trailhead, Killpecker Creek pours into the North Fork of the Poudre (which flows through the North Poudre Campground). The Killpecker Trail leads to the creek's headwaters about 2 miles south of the road. You'll find the best fishing in the lower reaches. Hike the trail roughly 0.5 mile upstream, then fish your way back down. A tiny mountain brook, Killpecker Creek flows through stands of pine and aspen where wildflowers grow. The streambed averages about 7 feet across. However, because much of it runs beneath deeply undercut banks, stretches of open water are only 3 to 5 feet wide. The creek's small size doesn't deter trout (including cutts, brookies, browns, and rainbows) from living there. Most are 8 to 10 inches long, but if you drift a nymph through one of the undercuts, you might hook a fish that's considerably larger. Especially from midsummer to early autumn, big browns and rainbows from the North Fork of the Poudre often swim up into Killpecker Creek to feed.

North Fork of the Cache la Poudre River, Upper Reaches

About 75 yards east of the Killpecker Trailhead and on the north side of Deadman Road, an unnamed four-wheel-drive road parallels the North Fork of the Poudre. The road heads downstream through an old-growth lodgepole pine forest for almost 0.4 mile on the river's east side. The road may be too rough for driving but it still makes a good trail. Follow it along the North Fork.

Upper stretches of the river move slowly. Pools and glides lie near deadfall and beaver dams; banks are earthen and undercut. Farther downstream, the water moves across a steeper streambed. There the North Fork quickens its pace and flows mostly in riffles and pockets. Streambanks become more rocky and sharply sloped. Trees and brush overhang much of the river, which measures about 10 to 15 feet wide. Because casting space is limited, you'll probably want to use a 6- to 7-foot rod. Whether you fish a dry fly or a nymph, concentrate on short-line presentations. On sunny midsummer days, watch for substantial emergences of yellow sally stoneflies, sizes #18 to #16.

NORTH FORK OF THE CACHE LA POUDRE RIVER, LOWER REACHES

(See map page 76.)

Management: USFS; CDOW; private.

Area maps: USFS map, Roosevelt and Arapaho national forests; CDOW map, Cherokee Park State Wildlife Area, Middle Unit; USGS map, Cherokee Park; DeLorme maps 20 and 19.

Average elevation: 6,900 feet.

Hiking distance: 1.1 miles.

Hike rating: Moderate to slightly difficult.

Special regulations: This stretch of river flows through the Cherokee Park State Wildlife Area Middle Unit, which is closed to public use from March 1 to Memorial Day. Fishing is restricted to catch-and-release with artificial flies or lures.

Directions: From Fort Collins, take U.S. 287 north to County Road 80C west. Drive 15.3 miles on County Road 80C, then turn right (north) into a fenced parking lot marked by a Colorado Division of Wildlife sign. Walk through the gate at the northeast corner of the parking lot. Walk south (back toward the road) about 200 yards on the trail that parallels the parking lot's eastern fence line. Then follow the trail east and south for about 20 minutes along a private-property fence line. This section of the trail makes a moderate ascent. At the trail's highest point, the river will come into view to the south. Hike down about 10 minutes more to reach the river. Note: Though well worn, the trail to the North Fork is not marked by signs. Be sure to bring a detailed map and a compass with you on this trip.

Once you reach the North Fork, you have a couple of options. You can work your way upstream, but after a few hundred yards, the river crosses private property. Regardless, even that short stretch of water might give you hours of good fishing. On the other hand, downstream reaches of the river flow within public lands for about 3 miles. Fishing there is as good as or better than it is upstream. Head upstream or down, you're still in a wilderness, and riverside trails are small, unmarked, and rough. The North Fork is about 30 feet wide, its flows varying from deep pools and broad runs to riffles and pockets. Submerged rocks and boulders form an uneven river bottom that's often difficult to wade. In addition, parts of the moderately sloped streambed are layered with silt. It's a good place to use a wading staff. Most of the trout are browns and rainbows from 10 to 14 inches long. Expect to see plenty of caddisflies; the green sedge (sizes #16 to #14) is especially prominent. Quill gordon, red quill, and blue-winged olive mayflies are common too. Terrestrial patterns produce well near shore.

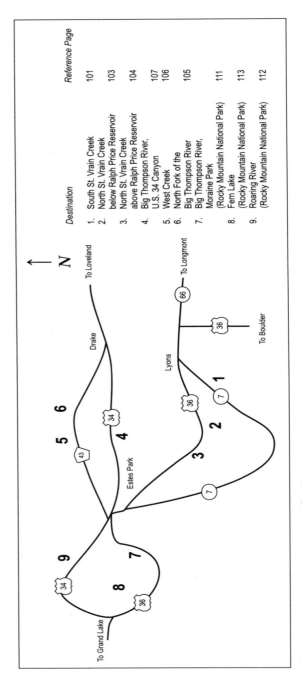

Destination		Reference Page
1.	South St. Vrain Creek	101
2.	North St. Vrain Creek below Ralph Price Reservoir	103
3.	North St. Vrain Creek above Ralph Price Reservoir	104
4.	Big Thompson River, U.S. 34 Canyon	107
5.	West Creek	106
6.	North Fork of the Big Thompson River	105
7.	Big Thompson River, Moraine Park	
8.	(Rocky Mountain National Park) Fern Lake	111
	(Rocky Mountain National Park)	113
9.	Roaring River (Rocky Mountain National Park)	112

Fig. 14. Loveland–Longmont Region

Chapter VI

LOVELAND–LONGMONT REGION

LOVELAND AND LONGMONT are cities of the plains, but a short drive west takes you to streams and rivers of mountain canyons. Fishing in canyons, particularly small ones, presents special considerations. For example, a cold stream flowing through a deep, narrow canyon receives little sunlight. Surface insect activity there generally remains subdued until the sun warms the area. In the cool of early morning, it's best to rely on wet flies and nymphs. Watch the south-facing shores for some of the day's first emergences.

Canyon walls can indicate the kind of water environment that flows by them. Sheer rock faces (which are often undercut) usually signify deep waters. Changes in the shape or slope of a canyon wall may mark variations in water types. If the remains of a rock slide are nearby, it's safe to assume that the stream bottom holds stones similar to those in the slide.

Dark rock retains more heat than light-colored rock. In cold-water canyons, trout often hold near dark-rock shores, especially after sunset. (In shallows, algae-coated streambed stones also absorb and hold heat.) On the other hand, if a canyon becomes unusually warm during the day, trout move away from the shoreline and into cooler, deeper places.

In a canyon, streamside vegetation such as grasses, willows, and other deciduous trees attracts not only terrestrial insects and bugs but also heavy concentrations of caddisflies and stoneflies; chances are trout will be near. Where yucca, cactus, and evergreen grow, a terrestrial pattern will probably produce better than an aquatic one.

SOUTH ST. VRAIN CREEK NEAR COLORADO 7
(See map page 100.)

Management: USFS; private.

Area maps: USFS map, Roosevelt and Arapaho national forests; USGS maps, Lyons and Raymond; DeLorme maps 30 and 29.

Average elevation: 6,500 feet.

Hiking distance: Most of the creek flows within 100 yards of the road.

Hike rating: Easy.

Special regulations: None.

Directions: From the junction of Colorado 7 and U.S. 36 in Lyons, take Colorado 7 west about 3.3 miles. The creek parallels the road for roughly 8 miles upstream toward the towns of Raymond and Riverside.

Averaging from 15 to 20 feet wide, the South St. Vrain flows mainly through the public lands of Roosevelt National Forest. The creek's riffled lower stretches follow a moderate grade. Upstream, the water steepens and courses through a narrow channel of plunge pools, chutes, and runs. The South St. Vrain is primarily a caddis water; green sedges are especially prolific. Streamside grasses are home to plenty of grasshoppers too. Herl-bodied flies, such as the dry-fly Western Coachman (sizes #16 to #12) and Prince Nymph (size #14 to #10), are among the most productive patterns. The Western Coachman is also effective when fished subsurface. Clinch weight onto the tippet about 6 inches above the fly and cast the pattern straight up-stream or up- and across-stream. Yarn or putty indicators on your leader will help you detect strikes. Whether you fish a dry fly or nymph, remember that on the South St. Vrain, short-line presentations are central to fly-fishing success.

Most anglers avoid fishing the creek's fastest and deepest waters, but those places typically hold the largest fish. Use a short leader tapered to 3X and place three or four BBs (or equivalent weight) on the tippet a few inches above the fly. A 20-Inch Nymph works well. After lobbing the weighted rig into the stream, keep your fly rod parallel to the water, but hold it high, at or above eye level. Keep a tight line as you watch your leader for a hint of a strike. With these kinds of presentations, the average drift might last only two or three seconds, and you're bound to lose some flies in the process. But when you do hook a fish, it will probably be a good one; like most mountain streams, the creek holds its share of pleasant surprises. From July through September, the creek's best dry-fly fishing usually occurs in the morning and early evening. During most summer afternoons, nymphs catch the most trout. Browns from 9 to 12 inches long are probably the most common trout in the creek, but brookies, rainbows, and an occasional cutt are present too.

NORTH ST. VRAIN CREEK DOWNSTREAM OF RALPH PRICE RESERVOIR
(See map page 100.)

Management: City of Longmont.

Area maps: USFS map, Roosevelt and Arapaho national forests; USGS map, Lyons; DeLorme maps 30 and 29.

Average elevation: 6,300 feet.

Hiking distance: 1.4 miles.

Hike rating: Easy.

Special regulations: None.

Directions: From the junction of Colorado 7 and U.S. 36 in Lyons, take U.S. 36 west about 3.8 miles. Turn left (south) on County Road 80 (Longmont Dam Road). Continue 2.7 miles to a locked steel gate and parking area. Then hike the road west along the creek. The road follows the North St. Vrain upstream for about 1.4 miles.

Although the creek runs through a steep-walled canyon, the streambed slopes gradually. Ponderosa pine and cactus grow on the rocky banks. In the broad, slack waters near Longmont Reservoir (about a 5-minute walk from the parking area), browns and rainbows often surface-feed on midges. The rest of the creek is about 30 feet wide and flows in riffles, pockets, and small pools. Whichever area you decide to fish, expect to see hatches of little brown stoneflies (sizes #18 to #16) during the spring and early summer. Midge patterns such as the Brassy and the Stuck-in-Shuck (sizes #22 to #20) produce well throughout the season. From summer through autumn, fair numbers of blue-winged olives (sizes #20 to #16) are active too. Watch for their spinner falls, especially in the late afternoon and evening.

NORTH ST. VRAIN CREEK UPSTREAM OF RALPH PRICE RESERVOIR
(See map page 100.)

Management: USFS; City of Longmont.

Area maps: USFS map, Roosevelt and Arapaho national forests; USGS maps, Panorama Peak, Raymond; DeLorme maps 30 and 29.

Elevations: Trailhead: 7,500 feet. Destination: 6,800 feet.

Hiking distance: 2.8 miles.

Hike rating: Slightly difficult.

Special regulations: Fishing is restricted to artificial flies or lures. The trout bag and possession limit is two fish.

Directions: From the junction of Colorado 7 and U.S. 36 in Lyons, take U.S. 36 west about 9.2 miles. Turn left (west and south) on County Road 47 (Big Elk Meadows Road). Travel 3 miles on County Road 47, then bear left (south) onto Forest Road 118. Follow Forest Road 118 0.4 mile to a parking area on the left (east) side of the road. USFS Trail #916 lies on the south side of the parking area. Hike the trail south to the creek.

At a moderate pace, your hike down to the North St. Vrain may take only an hour or so. Allow roughly twice that time for your return trip: In a little less than 3 miles, you'll need to climb about 700 feet. That may not sound too tough, but the sharpest ascent occurs in the last mile. Here's a quick look at the hike from trailhead to creek. After following the trail for about 30 minutes, you'll pass an old, roofless cabin near the trail's west side. The entrance to Button Rock Preserve lies a few minutes farther south. In the preserve, the trail becomes a grassy, four-wheel-drive road. From this point on to the water, the trail follows a much easier grade. Walk a few minutes more to a fork in the road. Stay on trail #916 by heading right (south). Continue to walk due south on the old road for about 20 minutes. Then you will arrive at a footbridge that crosses the creek.

This stretch of the North St. Vrain is a freestone mountain stream. Steep, rocky banks border a 20-foot-wide streambed that cuts through a canyon. Waters move in twisted currents around boulders and deadfall. Much of the creek flows in pockets and riffles, but deep, broad pools are common too. There's plenty of room to cast an 8- to 9-foot rod. Trout include browns and rainbows, as well as cutts, brookies, and cuttbows. The fish typically range from 10 to 14 inches long. Expect to see hatches and spinner falls of red quills and blue-winged olives. Green sedges and little spotted sedges are among the creek's most prevalent caddisflies. In addition, the North St. Vrain produces good emergences of yellow sallies and little green stoneflies. The streambed is home to a fair number of golden stonefly nymphs, sizes #6 to #2.

It's best (and easiest) to fish upstream of the bridge. On the creek's south side, you can walk on what's left of an unmarked jeep trail for about 0.4 mile. Then another bridge crosses the water and the trail continues almost a mile along the creek's north shore.

NORTH FORK OF THE BIG THOMPSON RIVER
(See map page 100.)

Management: USFS; National Park Service; private.

Area maps: USFS map, Roosevelt and Arapaho national forests; USGS maps, Glen Haven, Estes Park, Pingree Park; DeLorme map 29.

Elevations: Trailhead: 7,960 feet. Destination: 8,400 feet.

Hiking distance: 3 miles.

Hike rating: Moderate.

Special regulations: Within Rocky Mountain National Park, fishing is restricted to single-hook artificial flies or lures.

Directions: From Estes Park: From the intersection of U.S. 36 and U.S. 34, take the U.S. 34 Bypass (Wonderview Avenue) north and west about 0.4 mile. Turn right (north) on MacGregor Avenue, which becomes Devil's Gulch Road. Follow the road about 8.6 miles, then turn left (west) on County Road 51B.

From Loveland: Take U.S. 34 west to Drake and turn right on County Road 43. Follow County Road 43 about 5.9 miles, then turn right (west) on County Road 51B (Dunraven Glade Road), continue about 2.1 miles to a parking area and trailhead. Hike the North Fork Trail (#929) west and north to the river.

If you enjoy fishing small, wild waters, you'll probably love this beautiful little stretch of river. From the trailhead, it takes just 5 or 10 minutes to walk down a moderately steep grade that leads into the river canyon. When you arrive at the river, follow the trail upstream (to the west and north). The North Fork averages only about 10 feet wide and deadfall lies across much of its course. Trout (mostly brookies, rainbows, and browns) are rarely more than 8 to 10 inches long. Most of the North Fork flows fast, with plenty of riffles and plunge pools creating prime habitat for trout and aquatic insects. The Trude, Blue-Winged Olive, and Royal Wulff work well as dry flies. The best subsurface patterns include the Grizzly-and-Orange and 20-Inch Nymph; the streambed holds a large number of golden stoneflies.

A series of wooden bridges crosses the river as you follow the trail upstream. About 0.25 mile of the trail cuts through private property, where trespassing and fishing are prohibited. After crossing the sixth bridge, you'll enter a mountain meadow where a ramshackle cabin stands. Now known as Deserted Village, about a century ago the area was home to a hunting camp and several log buildings that have since fallen into ruin. Nearby, the streambanks steepen and the river flows in deeper pools. The Deserted Village site marks the end of this 3-mile hike and fishing trip. Farther upstream, the trail moves away from the water for about a mile, then follows the river more closely for about another 6.5 miles into Rocky Mountain National Park. If you'd like to make such a long trip into the backcountry, plan on camping, but check first with the National Park Service for necessary permits. The trail is also open to horse travel.

WEST CREEK
(See map page 100.)

Management: USFS; National Park Service.

Area maps: USFS map, Roosevelt and Arapaho national forests; Trails Illustrated, map 200; DeLorme map 29.

Elevations: Trailhead: 7,560 feet. Destination: 8,000 feet.

Hiking distance: 1.5 miles.

Hike rating: Moderate to slightly difficult.

Special regulations: Within Rocky Mountain National Park, fishing is restricted to single-hook artificial flies or lures.

Directions: From Estes Park: From the intersection of U.S. 36 and U.S. 34, take the U.S. 34 Bypass (Wonderview Avenue) north and west about 0.4 mile. Turn right (north) on MacGregor Avenue, which becomes Devil's Gulch Road. Follow the road about 3.3 miles, then bear left (north) on McGraw Ranch Road.

From Loveland: Take U.S. 34 west to Drake and turn right on County Road 43. Follow County Road 43 about 11.2 miles, then turn right (north) on McGraw Ranch Road.

Once you reach McGraw Ranch Road, drive about 2.1 miles to a roadside parking area. Walk a few hundred yards north to the North Boundary Trailhead and follow the trail north to the creek.

West Creek flows through a secluded, wooded valley that lies within Roosevelt National Forest and Rocky Mountain National Park. The trip from the trailhead to the creek takes around an hour. You'll spend about half that time climbing up the trail, and the other half descending it. When you reach the footbridge across the creek, you can hike the trail along the creek's north side. You might follow the trail upstream about 0.4 mile to its end at lovely West Creek Falls. Downstream of the bridge, you can walk the creekside trail almost 2 miles before the water enters private land. You probably won't need waders on either stretch. It's best to fish this little (12-foot-wide) creek with downstream presentations. A 7-foot rod with a 5- to 7-foot leader works well. Effective flies include the Stimulator, Red Quill, Caddis Larva, and Hare's Ear. The creek's small pools and glides often hold brown and brook trout up to 11 inches long.

BIG THOMPSON RIVER NEAR U.S. 34, BIG THOMPSON CANYON
(See map page 100.)

Management: USFS; private; City of Loveland; Larimer County.

Area maps: USFS map, Roosevelt and Arapaho national forests; Trails Illustrated Map 101; DeLorme maps 30 and 29.

Elevations: Upper reaches (near the Olympus dam): about 7,400 feet. Lower reaches (near the canyon outlet): about 5,400 feet.

Hiking distance: Most of the river flows within a few hundred yards of the road.

Hike rating: Easy.

Special regulations: From the Waltonia Bridge upstream to Gun Club Road, fishing is restricted to catch-and-release with artificial flies or lures.

Directions: From Estes Park: From the intersection of U.S. 36 and U.S. 34, take U.S. 34 east about 2 miles.

From Loveland: Take U.S. 34 west about 11 miles. U.S. 34 parallels most of the river.

Near the junction of U.S. 34 and U.S. 36 in Estes Park, the free-flowing waters of the Big Thompson River pour into Lake Estes, a man-made reservoir. At the lake's eastern end, the Olympus Dam releases water to the river downstream, though not in volumes large and regular enough to create a true, year-round tailwater fishery; in winter, nearly all of the river freezes. During much of the year, however, the Big Thompson downstream of the dam shows some characteristics that are reminiscent of a tailwater. For example, dam releases elevate the river's temperature, encouraging dense populations of midges and blue-winged olives. In addition, even when the upstream, wild-water stretches of the Big Thompson are high and roily, the river's regulated flows downstream of the dam may offer ideal fishing conditions.

The river moves along a sharp gradient, descending about 2,000 feet in its roughly 20-mile course through the scenic Big Thompson canyon. After a 1976 flood, many of the water's steep streambanks were reinforced with layers of large rocks, or rip-rap. Walking on rip-rap can be tricky; watch your step. In most places, wading the Big Thompson's rocky streambed is fairly easy. Much of the river runs in riffles, pocket waters, and plunge pools, and so lends itself well to short-line fishing.

Some of the river's prime fishing is found just east of the canyon, within areas owned or leased by the Sylvan Dale Guest Ranch, a resort located on U.S. 34 about 7 miles west of Loveland. The ranch lands and waters are private, and fishing there is restricted to guests or to anglers accompanied by an authorized guide. Rod fees are charged, and all fishing is limited to catch-and-release. The ranch also has several ponds, some of which hold large (over 5-pound) browns and rainbows.

Along U.S. 34 at the canyon's east entrance, about 2 miles of the river flow through the Narrows, an area defined by the sheer, rock sides of the canyon and the 50-foot-high concrete walls of the elevated roadway. There are a couple of access points down to the river (near the east and west ends of the Narrows), but the channeled streambed here does not provide particularly good habitat for trout. The Narrows is also a potentially dangerous place to fish, offering few routes of escape or places of shelter in the event of a sudden flood, water release, or thunderstorm.

In the 15 or so miles of water that lie upstream of the Narrows, many of the best fishing areas are those where the fewest people fish—in the canyon's lower and middle reaches. Located on the north side of U.S. 34, about 13.5 miles from Loveland and about 16 miles from Estes Park, is the Viestenz-Smith Mountain Park, which is managed by the City of Loveland. From the park about 2 miles upstream toward the Idylwild Dam, the river's plunge pools and pocket waters hold large populations of golden stonefly nymphs as well as many wild brown and rainbow trout.

From the Idylwild Dam upstream to Forks Park (in the town of Drake, near the river's confluence with the North Fork of the Big Thompson), the river has a similar character but flows in a generally broader course. Mayflies (including red quills, pale morning duns, and blue-winged olives) become more prominent, as do caddisflies such as the little autumn stream sedge and American grannom. Upstream of Forks Park to the Waltonia Bridge (which is about 19.2 miles west of Loveland and about 10.4 miles east of Estes Park), the river varies from about 15 to 30 feet across. Plunge pools, runs, and riffles appear with more frequency.

From Waltonia Bridge upstream about 5 miles to Gun Club Road, the Big Thompson is designated as a catch-and-release water. This stretch, a mix of runs, riffles, pocket water, and occasional glides, attracts the most fly anglers. There you'll find some of the river's heaviest hatches of midges and blue-winged olive mayflies, as well as some of the river's most heavily fished and spooky trout. The area from Gun Club Road upstream toward the Olympus Dam receives a fair bit of fishing pressure, too, especially during Estes Park's summer and early autumn tourist season.

A 3- to 5-weight, 8- to 9-foot rod with a 7- to 9-foot leader tapered to 5X or stouter is equal to most of the river's fly-fishing demands. The trout, mostly browns and rainbows, with a few cutts, average 10 to 13 inches long, though considerably larger fish (especially brown trout) are not unusual. Here's a list of some of the most popular fly patterns for the Big Thompson River.

Dry Flies:		*Nymphs:*	
Pattern	Size	Pattern	Size
Dry Midge	#22 to #18	Miracle Nymph	#22 to #18
Blue-Winged Olive	#22 to #16	Pheasant Tail	#22 to #18
Rusty Spinner	#20 to #16	Hare's Ear	#18 to #12
Deerhair Caddis (tan or olive)	#16 to #12	Prince Nymph	#18 to #12
Stimulator (orange)	#16 to #12	C.Q. Gordon	#16 to #12
		Orange Stone Nymph	#8 to #12
Hopper	#14 to #10		
Ant	#20 to #16	20-Inch Nymph	#8 to #12

ROCKY MOUNTAIN NATIONAL PARK

Home to towering mountains, flower-filled meadows, and prolific wildlife, Rocky Mountain National Park is recognized as one of the world's most spectacularly beautiful places. Each year it attracts more than three million visitors—most of them sightseers, not anglers. Almost two-thirds of the Park's 265,000 acres lie on the east side of the Continental Divide, only about an hour's drive from Boulder, Longmont, and Fort Collins. Despite its quality and accessibility, fly fishing in the park remains one of Colorado's best-kept angling secrets. Take a look at a few representative destinations described briefly here, and you'll probably want to spend some time fishing these and other nearby waters. For more detailed information and additional fly-fishing destinations, see the book *Fly Fishing Rocky Mountain National Park* (Hosman, 1996).

Entry into the national park requires a pass, which you can buy at an entrance station or visitor center. In 1998, a one-week pass cost $10, an annual pass $20. Camping is allowed only with a permit. Park maps and informational brochures are available free at the park's visitor centers. Some park waters (notably, those that hold greenback cutts) are restricted to catch-and-release fishing with single-hook artificial flies or lures. Where this restriction is not in effect, anglers twelve years of age or younger are allowed to fish with bait; all other anglers must fish exclusively with single-hook artificial flies or lures. Apart from these rules, general Colorado fishing regulations still apply.

Estes Park (elevation 7,500 feet) lies near the junction of U.S. 36 and U.S. 34, just east of the national park boundaries. Though small, the town has almost as many services as a city, including a hospital, supermarkets, restaurants, lodging, and shops. Estes Park's population of about 6,000 residents increases nearly tenfold during the summer tourist season, the height of which runs from Independence Day to Labor Day. To avoid crowds, plan your fishing trips for the early morning or early evening.

Big Thompson River, Moraine Park
(See map page 100.)

Management: National Park Service.

Area maps: Trails Illustrated Map 200; DeLorme map 29.

Elevation: 8,100 feet.

Hiking distance: Most of the river lies less than 0.5 mile from the road.

Hike rating: Easy.

Special regulations: Fishing is restricted to single-hook artificial flies or lures.

Directions: From the intersection of U.S. 36 and U.S. 34 in Estes Park, take U.S. 34 (Business) west through the center of town about 0.3 mile. Turn left (south and west) on U.S. 36. Follow U.S. 36 about 3.5 miles to the Beaver Meadows entrance. From the Beaver Meadows entrance, follow U.S. 36 about 0.2 mile. Turn left (south) on Bear Lake Road and continue about 1.6 miles. Turn right (west) into a parking area located next to the river.

Less than 50 yards upstream of the parking area, the river branches. For the best fishing, follow the right (north) fork upstream. This roughly 2-mile stretch of the Big Thompson holds brookies, browns, cutts, and rainbows. You might well catch one of each within a single run. The river measures about 15 to 20 feet across; many of its banks are deeply undercut. Apart from grasses, streamside vegetation is thin. Stay far from the banks as you walk through the moraine, and kneel or crouch at least a few feet away from the water when you cast. The Herl Nymph, Caddis Larva, and Rubber Band Nymph (sizes #16 to #12) are among the best subsurface patterns. Watch for hatches of blue-winged olives and red quills, along with substantial emergences of midges. In times of cold, fast-running flows, try fishing a dark Woolly Worm or Woolly Bugger down-and-across stream and close to the banks. The river takes on a much steeper gradient around the area of the Cub Lake trailhead, about 2 miles upstream from the parking area.

Roaring River
(See map page 100.)

Management: National Park Service.

Area maps: Trails Illustrated Map 200; DeLorme map 29.

Elevations: Trailhead: 8,500 feet. Destination: 9,300 feet.

Hiking distance: 1.5 miles.

Hike rating: Moderate to slightly difficult.

Special regulations: Fishing is restricted to catch-and-release with single-hook artificial flies or lures.

Directions: From the intersection of U.S. 36 and U.S. 34 in Estes Park, take U.S. 34 (Bypass) north and west about 4.8 miles to the Fall River entrance. From the Fall River entrance, follow Fall River Road west about 2.1 miles. Turn right (north) on Endovalley Road and drive about 0.1 mile to the Lawn Lake Trailhead parking area located on the right (east) side of the road. Hike the Lawn Lake Trail to Roaring River.

Much of the 800-foot elevation gain on the trail's route to the river occurs within the first 1.2 miles or so. If you're not accustomed to hiking at high altitudes, allow about 2 hours for the trip. Near the turnoff for the Ypsilon Lake Trail, a footbridge crosses Roaring River. As a rule, the best fishing lies upstream of the bridge. Roaring River's rocky banks are extremely unstable (as a result of a 1982 flood), and in places the water measures only about 10 feet wide. There's no need for waders, but an extra pair of dry socks might come in handy. Because of the river's high elevation, the prime dry-fly fishing usually occurs from late July through early September.

Nearly all the trout in Roaring River are greenback cutts, some over a foot long; rainbows are few. Keep low and cast a short line. Take the time to locate and observe trout, then try sightcasting to them. Many hold within the river's riffles and glides; others lurk by submerged rocks in pocket waters. Dry flies such as the Sofa Pillow, Colorado King, or Stimulator (sizes #14 to #10) can usually rise fish. The 20-Inch Nymph and Prince Nymph (sizes #16 to #10) work well subsurface.

Fern Lake
(See map page 100.)

Management: National Park Service.

Area maps: Trails Illustrated Map 200; DeLorme map 29.

Elevations: Trailhead: 8,200 feet. Destination: 9,500 feet.

Hiking distance: 4 miles.

Hike rating: Moderate to slightly difficult.

Special regulations: Fishing is restricted to catch-and-release with single-hook artificial flies or lures.

Directions: From the intersection of U.S. 36 and U.S. 34 in Estes Park, take U.S. 34 (Business) west through the center of town about 0.3 mile. Turn left (south and west) on U.S. 36. Follow U.S. 36 about 3.5 miles to the Beaver Meadows entrance. From the Beaver Meadows entrance, follow U.S. 36 about 0.2 mile. Turn left (south) on Bear Lake Road and continue about 1.3 miles. Turn right (west) on Moraine Park Campground Road and continue about 0.6 mile. Turn left (south) on Fern Lake Trailhead Road and drive 1.1 miles to the Fern Lake Trailhead parking area. Hike the Fern Lake Trail to Fern Lake.

Home to greenback cutts, this clear glacial lake covers 9 acres and attains a depth of nearly 35 feet. Fern Lake lies near two snowy peaks, the Little Matterhorn (to the south) and

Gabletop Mountain (to the west). Ice-out is usually complete by mid-July, with optimum fishing conditions occurring from early August through early September. The lake's eastern and southern shores, as well as areas near the inlet of Fern Creek, offer some of the best fishing. Wading is seldom necessary: The cutts (most between 10 to 13 inches long) often cruise close to the shorelines as they search for food. Most of the lake has a rocky bottom, but deep deposits of silt lie near the banks. Effective dry flies include dark ant patterns, sizes #20 to #16; Blue-Winged Olive, sizes #20 to #16; and Parachute Emerger, sizes #22 to #18. For a nymph, try a Bead-head Hare's Ear or a Partridge-and-Orange, sizes #18 to #16. An 8- to 9-foot, 4-weight rod and 10-foot leader provide delicate presentations as well as the power to contend with frequent breezes.

Chapter VII
LONGMONT–BOULDER REGION

MORE THAN HALF of this region's fly-fishing destinations lie near the magnificent Indian Peaks Wilderness Area within Roosevelt National Forest. Elevations there are typically above 10,000 feet. You'll be fishing near the treeline where, even in midsummer, snowfields are common. In this subalpine environment, insects, like wildflowers, appear later in the season—but in greater profusion—than they do at lower elevations. During the cold-water months of June and July, nymph fishing is usually most productive. By the beginning of August and for a few weeks afterward, water temperatures in streams and lakes finally begin to warm. That relatively brief period produces intense emergences of mayflies, midges, caddis, and stoneflies. Then the quality of dry-fly fishing often rates as nothing less than fantastic; enjoy it while you can.

On some days in late summer, adult midges and midge shucks may cover the entire surface of a high-mountain lake. It's easy to mistake the filmy mass of insects for a low-lying fog. Bring plenty of midge patterns, including the Stuck-in-Shuck, Stillborn Emerger, and Parachute Emerger. Dry-fly ants and beetles can be extremely effective too; upslope winds often carry swarms of terrestrials from lower elevations to higher ones. When the wind blows, concentrate your presentations near the leeward shores; they accumulate the most foods. Also look for sheltered spots (in coves, around deadfall, and so on) where trout hold when the water gets choppy. Whatever the weather conditions when fishing a high mountain lake, be patient. Very patient. Sometimes the best presentation is simply the one that stays on the water for the longest time.

BRAINARD LAKE
(See map page 116.)

Management: USFS.

Area maps: USFS map, Roosevelt and Arapaho national forests; Trails Illustrated map 102; DeLorme map 29.

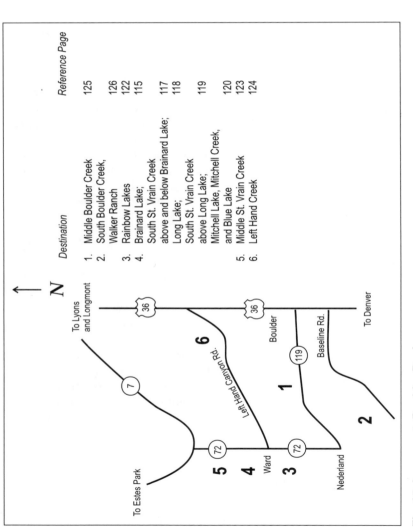

Fig. 15. Longmont–Boulder Region

	Destination	Reference Page
1.	Middle Boulder Creek	125
2.	South Boulder Creek,	126
	Walker Ranch	122
3.	Rainbow Lakes	115
4.	Brainard Lake;	
	South St. Vrain Creek	
	above and below Brainard Lake;	117
	Long Lake;	118
	South St. Vrain Creek	
	above Long Lake;	119
	Mitchell Lake, Mitchell Creek,	
	and Blue Lake	
5.	Middle St. Vrain Creek	120
6.	Left Hand Creek	123
		124

Elevation: 10,300 feet.

Hiking distance: Most of the lake lies less than a few hundred yards from the road.

Hike rating: Easy.

Special regulations: None.

Directions: From Boulder, take Colorado 119 south to Colorado 72 west and north. About 0.25 mile north of the town of Ward, turn left (west) on Forest Road 112 toward the Brainard Lake Recreation Area. Continue about 5 miles to Brainard Lake.

Because a paved road and parking areas are nearby, Brainard is one of the few high mountain lakes where you can fish an evening rise without having to camp overnight. Look for the best fishing at the lake's west end, near the inlets of the Mitchell and South St. Vrain creeks. Rainbows, browns, and brookies usually hold in or near the currents created by the two streams. Midge activity is often intense; you might also see long-horn sedges alighting on or flying near the water. Try fishing a two-fly rig: a size #12 Colorado King or Stimulator with a size #22 Stuck-in-Shuck as a dropper about 18 inches below the dry fly. Use a dead-drift presentation, but if a trout doesn't strike, twitch the flies slightly about every five to ten seconds. Remember that especially in still waters, trout tend to hit a fly just as it appears to be moving out of reach.

SOUTH ST. VRAIN CREEK ABOVE AND BELOW BRAINARD LAKE
(See map page 116.)

Management: USFS.

Area maps: USFS map, Roosevelt and Arapaho national forests; Trails Illustrated map 102; DeLorme map 29.

Average elevation: 10,370 feet.

Hiking distance: 1 mile.

Hike rating: Easy to moderate.

Special regulations: Downstream of Brainard Lake, there are none. However, from Brainard Lake upstream to the creek's headwaters, fishing is restricted to artificial flies or lures; the trout bag and possession limit is two fish. In addition, the South

St. Vrain Creek between Long Lake and Brainard Lake is closed to fishing from May 1 to July 15.

Directions: From Boulder, take Colorado 119 south to Colorado 72 west and north. About 0.25 mile north of the town of Ward, turn left (west) on Forest Road 112 toward the Brainard Lake Recreation Area. Continue about 5 miles to Brainard Lake.

The lower reaches of the creek lie on the lake's east (outlet) end. Parking areas are nearby. A path along the stream's east side follows the water downstream. Upper reaches of the creek flow a few hundred yards south of the turnoff for the Long Lake Trailhead. From the east end of Brainard Lake, follow the road west about 0.3 mile to roadside parking areas. Unmarked trails parallel the creek upstream toward Long Lake.

A 0.7-mile stretch of the South St. Vrain pours from Long Lake down to Brainard Lake. It then drains out of Brainard and runs almost 6 miles before crossing private land. Lodgepole forest surrounds much of the creek, which flows in riffles, glides, and pockets. Below Brainard Lake, water temperatures average about 5 degrees higher than they do in the upstream reaches. When fishing downstream of Brainard, avoid walking on the west banks: vegetation there conceals old barbed wire. Though small (about 10 to 20 feet across), the creek holds cutts, rainbows, browns, and brookies, most from 8 to 12 inches long. Useful patterns include the Parachute Emerger (sizes #22 to #20) and the Grizzly-and-Orange (sizes #18 to #16).

LONG LAKE
(See map page 116.)

Management: USFS.

Area maps: USFS map, Roosevelt and Arapaho national forests; Trails Illustrated map 102; DeLorme map 29.

Elevations: Trailhead: 10,480 feet. Destination: 10,520 feet.

Hiking distance: 0.25 mile.

Hike rating: Easy.

Special regulations: Fishing is restricted to artificial flies or lures. The trout bag and possession limit is two fish.

Directions: From Boulder, take Colorado 119 south to Colorado 72 west and north. About 0.25 mile north of the town of

Ward, turn left (west) on Forest Road 112 toward the Brainard Lake Recreation Area. Continue about 5 miles to Brainard Lake. From the east end of Brainard Lake, follow the road west about 0.3 mile and turn at the parking area for the Long Lake Trailhead. Hike the trail to the lake.

Long Lake covers about 40 acres, its rocky bottom sloping to depths of nearly 20 feet. It's a wonderful place to float-tube, though shore fishing can be productive too, particularly in the early morning and evening. Like Brainard Lake, Long Lake produces dense emergences of midges, sizes #30 to #20. Try casting to rising trout with a Parachute Emerger or Hill's Stillborn Emerger, sizes #26 to #18. Larger, subsurface patterns such as the Cranefly Larva, Woolly Bugger, and Little Brook Trout (sizes #12 to #8) perform well when fished slowly and deep.

SOUTH ST. VRAIN CREEK ABOVE LONG LAKE
(See map page 116.)

Management: USFS.

Area maps: USFS map, Roosevelt and Arapaho national forests; Trails Illustrated map 102; DeLorme map 29.

Average elevation: 10,600 feet.

Hiking distance: 1 mile.

Hike rating: Moderate to slightly difficult.

Special regulations: Fishing is restricted to artificial flies or lures. The trout bag and possession limit is two fish.

Directions: From Boulder, take Colorado 119 south to Colorado 72 west and north. About 0.25 mile north of the town of Ward, turn left (west) on Forest Road 112 toward the Brainard Lake Recreation Area. Continue about 5 miles to Brainard Lake. From the east end of Brainard Lake, follow the road west about 0.3 mile and turn at the parking area for the Long Lake Trailhead. Hike the trail to the lake. From the east end of Long Lake, hike the Pawnee Pass Trail west along the lake's northern shore. The South St. Vrain flows into the west end of Long Lake. Deer trails and foot paths near the creek follow its course upstream. The Pawnee Pass Trail parallels the creek too, but at a distance of a few hundred yards from the water.

Though located above 10,000 feet, most of this stretch of the South St. Vrain creek runs along a fairly easy grade. Near Long Lake, the streamside vegetation is about waist-high and exceptionally thick. Hiking and wading become easier a few hundred yards upstream, where banks are grassy and willow-lined. Much of the 15- to 20-foot-wide creek flows in riffles. Caddisflies (including the little autumn stream sedge, long-horn sedge, and green sedge) thrive there. Either a Deerhair Caddis (sizes #16 to #12) or a Henryville Special (size #16) makes a good choice for a dry fly. Blue-winged olives and slate-winged olives (sizes #18 to #14) are among the most common mayflies. In midsummer, expect to see some little brown stoneflies too. The creek holds mainly brookies, rainbows, and cutts, as well as an occasional brown trout. The fish range from 9 to 12 inches long. If you follow the South St. Vrain upstream about a mile beyond Long Lake, you'll arrive at Lake Isabelle. Though 10 acres smaller than Long Lake, Isabelle is nearly twice as deep and offers comparable fishing. Roughly another mile to the west and south, the headwaters of the South St. Vrain pour from the Isabelle Glacier.

MITCHELL LAKE, MITCHELL CREEK, AND BLUE LAKE
(See map page 116.)

Management: USFS.

Area maps: USFS map, Roosevelt and Arapaho national forests; Trails Illustrated map 102; DeLorme map 29.

Elevations: Trailhead: 10,480 feet. Mitchell Lake: 10,720 feet; Mitchell Creek: 11,000 feet, average; Blue Lake: 11,320 feet.

Hiking distances: Mitchell Lake: 0.5 mile. Mitchell Creek: 0.7 mile. Blue Lake: 3 miles.

Hike ratings: Easy to slightly difficult, depending on the distance traveled.

Special regulations: None.

Directions: From Boulder, take Colorado 119 south to Colorado 72 west and north. About 0.25 mile north of the town of Ward, turn left (west) on Forest Road 112 toward the Brainard Lake Recreation Area. Continue about 5 miles to Brainard Lake. From the east end of Brainard Lake, follow the road west about 0.3 mile and turn at the parking area for the Mitchell Creek Trailhead. The trail leads to Mitchell Lake, Mitchell Creek, and Blue Lake.

The hike to Mitchell Lake takes about 20 minutes, the trail leading near Mitchell's rocky southern shores. Keep low to the ground as you approach the water and you'll likely see cutts cruising in the shallows. Expect to find the best fishing in the eastern two-thirds of the lake, as well as in and around the western inlet. Count on midge patterns (such as the Parachute Emerger, Hill's Stillborn Emerger, and Dale's Midge Larva, sizes #24 to #20) to catch the most trout. Mitchell Lake covers nearly 15 acres and it reaches a maximum depth of around 10 feet.

At the lake's west end, brilliantly colored wildflowers bloom in midsummer on the banks of Mitchell Creek. To follow the trail toward Blue Lake, you'll need to cross the creek, either by wading or by walking on a rickety log footbridge. In high-water times, parts of the bridge may be submerged. For the next mile or so, Mitchell Creek flows in riffles but occasionally runs through small, ponded wetlands where both midges and mosquitoes thrive. The creek varies in width from 10 to 20 feet across. It's home to cutts, brookies, and rainbows, most of them less than 11 inches long. The streambed's moderate slope steepens as you head closer to Blue Lake.

The last few hundred yards of the trail to Blue Lake follow a rough route that takes you near a small snowfield. Lichens, primrose, and stunted spruce trees grow in the near-alpine terrain. In the distance to the northwest, a little stream cascades down the mountainside. Climb over the last rise in the trail and Blue Lake comes into view. Mountain peaks nearly 13,000 feet high rise to the lake's north, south, and west. The lake spreads across 26 acres and, in places, measures 100 feet deep. Trout, including rainbows and cutts, often hold near the north shore and outlet. Because of loose rock, snowfields, and sheer rock faces, much of the lake's southern and western shores are difficult or impossible to traverse. The Brassy and Hill's Stillborn Emerger (sizes #22 to #18) are productive flies in Blue Lake, as are surface and subsurface ant patterns, sizes #24 to #16. Plan on using a 9- to 10-foot leader, and to contend with winds, at least a 4-weight line.

RAINBOW LAKES
(See map page 116.)

Management: USFS.

Area maps: USFS map, Roosevelt and Arapaho national forests; Trails Illustrated map 102; DeLorme map 29.

Elevations: Trailhead: 9,960 feet. Destination: 10,200 feet.

Hiking distance: 0.5 mile.

Hike rating: Easy.

Special regulations: None.

Directions: From Boulder, take Colorado 119 south to Colorado 72 west and north. About 7 miles north of the town of Nederland, turn left (west) on Forest Road 298, which is marked by a sign for the University of Colorado Mountain Research Station. Follow the road about 5 miles to the Rainbow Lakes Trailhead. Note: Though graded, Forest Road 298 is often rough. If you can, travel there by truck.

The Rainbow Lakes comprise about ten small lakes, the best two of which are located about a 45-minute walk from the Rainbow Lakes Trailhead. As you hike on the tree-lined trail, you'll pass a few of the lower lakes. Generally weedy and silted, they don't have particularly good fishing. However, some of the small creeks that flow near and across the trail are home to large numbers of brook trout. The trail dwindles to its end in a small boulder field. Within view to the north is a roughly 1.5-acre, 8-foot deep lake; just yards away over a small rise to the south lies a larger lake of about twice that size and depth. Both hold 8- to 10-inch brook trout. Though small, the fish can be surprisingly selective and difficult to catch. To fool them, you'll often need tiny (sizes #26 to #22) midge patterns, such as the Stuck-in-Shuck and Dale's Midge Larva; 12-foot leaders and 7X tippets may help too. Sometimes, though, trout will strike at practically any fly. I don't know why.

Several years ago, during a morning of difficult fishing on the upper south lake in late July, a cold wind suddenly blew from the east. The sky darkened, and moments later, a 3-foot-high waterspout swirled for several seconds around the lake's northeast corner. Hail and lightning followed, lasting the better part of an hour. When the storm subsided, my friends and I left our shelters in the low pines nearby and got ready to start fishing again. Standing ankle-deep in the hailstones that covered the shoreline, we saw fish rising throughout the lake. For the next couple of hours, trout took nearly every fly we cast, no matter how outrageous the patterns or how terrible our presentations. Then all became quiet again. There's a limit to fly-fishing logic. But when you fish the upper Rainbow Lakes, just be sure to bring lots of midges. And look out for those waterspouts.

MIDDLE ST. VRAIN CREEK
(See map page 116.)

Management: USFS; private.

Area maps: USFS map, Roosevelt and Arapaho national forests; Trails Illustrated map 102; DeLorme map 29.

Average elevation: 8,900 feet.

Hiking distance: 1 mile.

Hike rating: Easy to moderate.

Special regulations: None.

Directions: From Boulder, take Colorado 119 south to Colorado 72 west and north. About 6 miles north of the town of Ward, turn left (west) on County Road 92, which is marked by a sign indicating Peaceful Valley Campground and Camp Dick. The paved road follows the creek about 1.2 miles. Then Forest Road 114, a rough four-wheel-drive trail, parallels the south side of the creek for about 4 miles.

The land around the creek, like the water itself, is rich in life. Moss, a relative rarity in Front Range terrain, grows along the streambanks, as does a profusion of wildflowers. Aspen and old-growth evergreens line the banks, some of the trees lying in deadfall across the water. In places near the campgrounds, streamside vegetation is dense; hiking through it can be slow going. However, you can walk along the road until you find a clearing to the water. Keep an eye out for bears; the campgrounds attract them.

Close by the Peaceful Valley Campground, the creek flows in two small branches of riffles, small pools, and backwaters.

The area has good fishing, but little room for casting. Camp Dick is located about a mile upstream, and there the creek broadens, flowing in a single cascading channel of slicks, runs, pools, and riffles. Upstream of Camp Dick, there is a footpath and a four-wheel-drive road (Forest Road 114) that parallels the creek's south side. Buchanan Pass Trail (#910) follows the creek along its north side. Most of the stream is between 15 and 20 feet wide.

Because many of the Middle St. Vrain's lower reaches are brushy and narrow, bring a fly rod that measures 8 feet or less. In summer, try using an 8-foot leader tapered to 4X or 5X; longer leaders become useful during the low-water times of the early and late season. Whatever the time of year, work the pockets around boulders, the sun-dappled riffles, and the lines of foam and bubbles near shore. Don't overlook the deep pools, the slick flows beneath the overhanging willows, and the creases of water right next to the streambank. With good technique and the right fly, you'll catch trout.

Some of the best dry flies include the Quill Gordon (sizes #14 to #12); yellow-brown or olive Deerhair Caddis or Henryville Special (sizes #16 to #12); and Blue-Winged Olive (sizes #18 to #14). The C.Q. Gordon (sizes #16 to #12) is an especially effective nymph. The creek also holds an unusually high number of aquatic moth larvae. Pale to dark olive in color, they range in size from 8 to 16 mm long (hook sizes #16 to #10). Their best all-round imitation: a Woolly Worm. With luck, though, you should be able to fish dry flies exclusively throughout most of the summer and autumn. Brown trout dominate the fish population, but brookies, rainbows, and cutts are present too, most of them measuring between 9 and 11 inches long.

LEFT HAND CREEK
(See map page 116.)

Management: City of Boulder; USFS; private.

Area maps: USFS map, Roosevelt and Arapaho national forests; USGS map, Boulder; DeLorme maps 30 and 29.

Average elevation: 6,640 feet.

Hiking distance: Most of the creek lies within a few hundred yards of the road.

Hike rating: Easy.

Special regulations: None.

Directions: From Boulder, take U.S. 36 north. About 7 miles from the intersection of U.S. 36 and Colorado 119, turn left (west and south) on Left Hand Canyon Drive. Follow the road about 2.4 miles to Buckingham Park. From that point upstream, most of the creek is open to the public for nearly 3 miles.

Left Hand Creek offers a fun, small-stream getaway that's close to Boulder. Willow, pine, and sunflowers grow along the steep banks, and net-spinning caddis abound on the rocky streambed. Browns, rainbows, and brookies are common in the creek's clear, fast waters, though occasionally you'll catch cutts and cuttbows too. The stream is about 15 feet wide—best for short-line, pocket-water fishing.

MIDDLE BOULDER CREEK
(See map page 116.)

Management: USFS; private.

Area maps: USFS map, Roosevelt and Arapaho national forests; USGS maps, Boulder, Gold Hill, Tungsten; DeLorme maps 39 and 29.

Average elevation: 6,750 feet.

Hiking distance: Most of the creek lies within a few hundred yards of the road.

Hike rating: Easy.

Special regulations: None.

Directions: From Boulder, take Canyon Boulevard (Colorado 119) west into Roosevelt National Forest. The National Forest boundary lies about 6.5 miles from the intersection of Canyon Boulevard and Broadway (Colorado 93) in Boulder. Upstream of the boundary, the creek flows near the road through both public and private lands for nearly 8 miles.

Only about a 20-minute drive from downtown Boulder, this stretch of Middle Boulder Creek holds small, wild trout, and lots of them. Brookies are most prevalent, but browns, cutts, and rainbows live there as well. The fish typically keep close to the banks and near submerged boulders, deadfall, and other shelter. The creek averages from 20 to 25 feet wide. The relatively sparse streamside vegetation seldom interferes with casting, even if you're using a fairly long rod. In summer, trout rise to all-purpose dry flies such as the Adams and Stimulator, sizes #18 to #14. Try fishing the riffles and pools with down-and-across presentations of an olive Hare's Ear or Caddis Larva, sizes #16 to #12.

SOUTH BOULDER CREEK, WALKER RANCH
(See map page 116.)

Management: Boulder County; Denver Water Board; Bureau of Land Management; private.

Area maps: USFS map, Roosevelt and Arapaho national forests; USGS map, Eldorado Springs; DeLorme maps 30 and 29.

Elevations: Trailhead: 7,200 feet. Destination: 6,680 feet.

Hiking distance: 1.1 miles.

Hike rating: Moderate to slightly difficult.

Special regulations: None.

Directions: From Boulder, head west on Baseline Road, which merges into Flagstaff Road. Follow Flagstaff Road through Boulder Mountain Park. About 0.3 mile past the Meyers Gulch picnic area (located on the right side of the road), turn left (south) at the parking area for the South Boulder Creek Trailhead. Hike the trail south to the creek.

On your drive to the ranch, you may want to stop along Flagstaff Road to take in the panoramic views of Boulder and the plains beyond. At a moderate pace, it takes about 40 minutes to walk from the trailhead to the creek. Along the route, the trail descends nearly 500 feet. If the slope doesn't seem bad during your trip down to the water, it probably will when you hike back up to the trailhead. The trail, bordered by sparse scrub pine, yucca, and prickly pear cactus, crosses mostly open country and offers little protection from the sun and wind. Walker Ranch is a popular place for backcountry cyclists; watch out for them along trails and roadways.

Near the creek, the trail heads generally west and follows

the water upstream. Begin fishing there if you like, but downstream reaches are worth exploring. Hike for another half-hour or so, following the water downstream on an unmarked but well-worn footpath on the creek's north side. In places, this stretch of the creek is more than 40 feet across, with plenty of room for casting and opportunities for long-line presentations. Fish your way back upstream toward the main trail, where another mile or so of fast waters and glides flow.

The creek has a robust variety of aquatic insects, including substantial populations of red quills, quill gordons, and blue-winged olives. The stream is so vibrant that on a single 50-foot stretch, several hatches and falls might occur in less than an hour. Whatever kind of mayfly dun is active, try using an olive Comparadun in a size to match the natural insect. Focus your presentations within the slicks, runs, and edgewaters where the fish will most likely be rising. The Rusty Spinner (sizes #18 to #14) and Parachute Emerger (sizes #18 to #16) also will prove worthwhile.

South Boulder Creek holds browns and rainbows, many over 11 inches long. You may catch small brookies and a few fair-sized cutts too. The stream has some deep and fast-moving sections, but it's generally easy to wade. If you're not accustomed to physical exertion at high elevations, allow the better part of an hour for your hike back up to the trailhead.

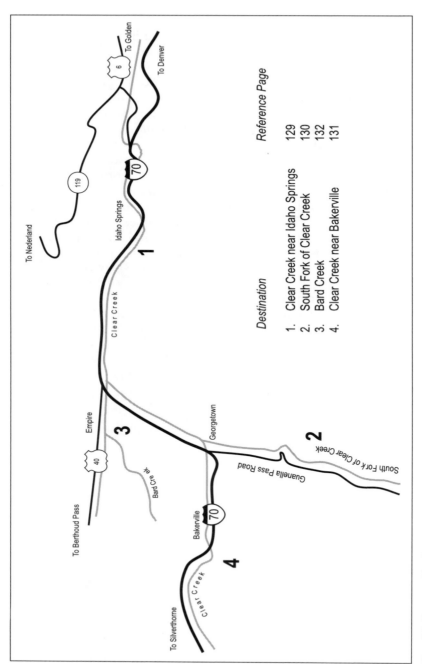

Fig. 16. Denver Region

Chapter VIII
DENVER REGION

CLEAR CREEK COUNTY, just west of Denver, was still part of the Kansas Territory when prospectors found gold there in 1858. During the mining boom that followed, mountainsides were torn open and stripped of trees; tailings poisoned streams. Though many waters in the region (including parts of Fall River, and the North and West Forks of Clear Creek) may look appealing, they remain seriously damaged by the effects of mining. But a few streams have again become viable trout habitats; Clear Creek and Bard Creek are prime examples. Nearby cities and towns have undergone a renaissance too. Places such as Idaho Springs, Georgetown, and Empire offer not only lodging, shops, and restaurants, but some of the most charming Victorian architecture in Colorado. For information on backcountry conditions, stop by the U.S. Forest Visitor's Center in Idaho Springs. It's located near I-70 exit 240.

CLEAR CREEK NEAR IDAHO SPRINGS
(See map page 128.)

Management: Bureau of Land Management; private.

Area maps: USFS map, Roosevelt and Arapaho national forests; Trails Illustrated maps 103 and 104; DeLorme map 39.

Average elevation: 8,160 feet.

Hiking distance: Most of the creek flows within a hundred yards of the road.

Hike rating: Easy.

Special regulations: None.

Directions: From Denver, take I-70 west to exit 240 for Mount Evans. At the end of the exit ramp, turn right on 13th Avenue. Follow 13th Avenue a few blocks north, then turn left (west) on Colorado Boulevard. Continue west on Colorado Boulevard roughly 0.8 mile, then bear left on Stanley Road, which crosses

Clear Creek. Drive about 2.5 miles on Stanley Road. From that point on upstream, Stanley Road parallels public sections of Clear Creek for nearly 2 miles.

Though located within view of mine sites, tailings, and an interstate highway, this section of Clear Creek has somehow retained its vitality. Waters flow in plunge pools, slicks, and riffles across a rocky streambed. The creek is about 30 feet wide and in places measures well over 4 feet deep. Willows, grasses, and black-eyed Susans grow along the gently sloping south bank. Most of the north bank is sharply inclined and unstable. On a summer afternoon, you'll often see dozens of swallows swooping toward the creek's surface. The event signals a concentrated presence of aquatic insects, usually mayflies or caddisflies. Caddis (including the green sedge and tan short-horn sedge) are common in and around the creek; most range in size from #18 to #14. Blue-winged olives (sizes #20 to #16) probably rate as the most prevalent mayfly, but from time to time, substantial hatches of green drakes also occur. Much of this stretch of Clear Creek flows through public acreage administered by the Bureau of Land Management (BLM). However, be sure to watch for and to respect boundaries of adjoining private properties.

SOUTH FORK OF CLEAR CREEK NEAR GUANELLA PASS CAMPGROUND
(See map page 128.)

Management: USFS; private.

Area maps: USFS map, Roosevelt and Arapaho national forests; Trails Illustrated map 104; DeLorme map 39.

Average elevation: 10,560 feet.

Hiking distance: Most sections of the creek lie a few hundred yards from the road.

Hike rating: Easy.

Special regulations: None.

Directions: From Denver, take I-70 west to exit 228 for Georgetown. Follow the signs in Georgetown to Guanella Pass Road. The best stretches of the creek lie upstream of the turnoff for the Clear Lake campground, about 6.5 miles from the center of Georgetown.

A picture-perfect little trout stream, the South Fork winds through a high mountain meadow where wild roses bloom. On a midsummer day, it's a delightful place to cast a cane rod for brookies. Willows grow along the grassy, undercut banks and the water is remarkably clear. Much of the creek (which averages from 12 to 15 feet wide) flows in riffles, glides, and runs. Ponded sections, created by an active population of beavers, are common too. Fishing is best in the roughly 3-mile stretch from the Clear Lake Campground upstream toward the Guanella Pass Campground. Terrestrial patterns (such as ants, hoppers, and beetles) work well as dry flies.

CLEAR CREEK NEAR BAKERVILLE
(See map page 128.)

Management: USFS; private.

Area maps: USFS map, Roosevelt and Arapaho national forests; Trails Illustrated map 104; DeLorme map 38.

Average elevation: 10,000 feet.

Hiking distance: Most of the creek flows within a few hundred yards of the Bakerville–Loveland Trail (formerly Forest Road 730). When completed in 2000 or 2001, the trail will parallel the south side of the creek for about 4.7 miles. Note: At this writing, the USFS is considering renaming the Bakerville–Loveland Trail, which some maps now indicate as "BLT Trail," or simply "BLT." The Forest Service apparently has two concerns. First, people might think that "Loveland" referred to the city, not to the mountain pass. And that "BLT" would become the first USFS trail to have the same name as a sandwich.

Hike rating: Easy to difficult, depending on the distance you choose to hike.

Special regulations: None.

Directions: From Denver, take I-70 west to exit 221 for Bakerville. Follow the exit ramp south over I-70 to Clear Creek. The Bakerville–Loveland Trail heads west as it parallels the south side of the creek.

What an odd place to fish. South of the creek lie miles of wilderness, the peak of Mount Sniktau, and the Continental Divide. But just a few hundred yards to the north, traffic roars by on Interstate 70. However, the stream itself is still wild. Thick groves of aspen, juniper, and pine grow along the marshy south shore. In and near the streambed, you'll see beaver dams and lodges. The water's amazing clarity belies its depth: More often than not, water that appears only knee-deep is actually waist-high. The creek produces varied water-types and trout habitat. In one stretch, you might cast into 100-foot-long, 40-foot-wide riffles; in the next, into narrow, undercut runs overhung with willows. In most areas, Clear Creek is from 12 to 20 feet across. Watch for the hatches and falls of red quills and quill gordons, as well as numerous kinds of caddisflies. Hopper patterns produce well in summer and early autumn. The trout (mostly cutts, rainbows, and brookies) generally measure between 9 and 11 inches long.

BARD CREEK
(See map page 128.)

Management: USFS; private.

Area maps: USFS map, Roosevelt and Arapaho national forests; Trails Illustrated Map 103; DeLorme map 39.

Average elevation: 10,000 feet.

Hiking distance: 1 mile.

Hike rating: Moderate.

Special regulations: Fishing is restricted to catch-and-release with artificial flies or lures.

Directions: From Denver, take I-70 west to exit 232 for Empire. Follow U.S. 40 to the center of Empire and turn left (south) on Bard Creek Road. Follow Bard Creek Road about 4.3 miles to the Bard Creek Trail (#83), which parallels the stream. Note: South of Empire Pass (around 2.3 miles from town), the road forks twice. Bear right (north) at each fork. The road then heads west and southwest and stays near the creek. At Empire Pass, the road gets rough. Travel this stretch of Bard Creek Road by hiking, horseback riding, mountain biking, or driving a high-clearance, four-wheel-drive vehicle. Don't try to make the trip in a typical passenger car.

The area around Bard Creek is rugged, wild, and seldom used. Near the entrance sign for Arapaho National Forest (about 2.5 miles from Empire), the USFS maintains a visitor logbook. Take a minute to note your name and destination, as well as the times of your arrival and departure. On the way to the Bard Creek Trail (1.8 miles past the entrance sign), you'll drive through about 0.5 mile of private land, passing an old mine site and piles of tailings on the road's north side. The Bard Creek Trail generally keeps at least a hundred yards or so from the water. The creek courses through thick evergreen forest and near boulder fields. Hiking there can be slow and tedious. As you walk by the creek, you may come across a run-down cabin or two, a sawmill site, and other relics of Colorado mining history. Bard Creek is tiny and brushy. It occasionally flows into pools and glides, but in most places, the water measures only 5 to 8 feet across. The good news: Greenback cutts thrive there. You'll probably find it easiest to fish the creek with a short (5- to 6-foot) rod and leader. Because of limited casting space, plan on making most of your presentations with roll-casts; dapping and skittering techniques also work well. Chartreuse Trudes and medium-olive Cahills, sizes #18 to #14, are especially productive as dry flies. The Bard Creek Trail follows the creek for about 4 miles, the last three of which are extremely steep and difficult.

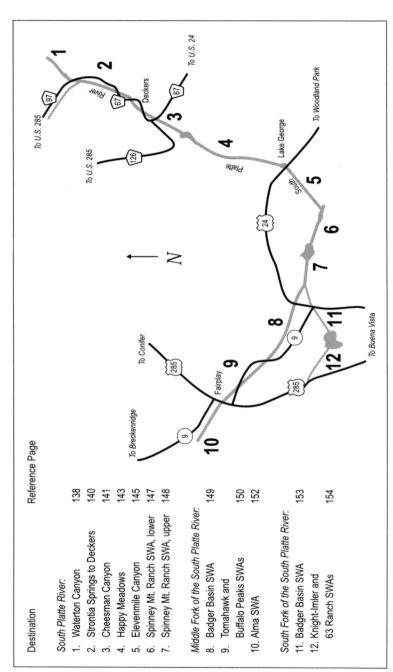

Destination	Reference Page
South Platte River:	
1. Waterton Canyon	138
2. Strontia Springs to Deckers	140
3. Cheesman Canyon	141
4. Happy Meadows	143
5. Elevenmile Canyon	145
6. Spinney Mt. Ranch SWA, lower	147
7. Spinney Mt. Ranch SWA, upper	148
Middle Fork of the South Platte River:	
8. Badger Basin SWA	149
9. Tomahawk and	
Buffalo Peaks SWAs	150
10. Alma SWA	152
South Fork of the South Platte River:	
11. Badger Basin SWA	153
12. Knight-Imler and	
63 Ranch SWAs	154

Fig. 17. Denver–Colorado Springs Region: South Platte River

Chapter IX

DENVER–COLORADO SPRINGS REGION: THE SOUTH PLATTE RIVER

" . . . and certainly as some Pastures do
breed larger Sheep, so do some Rivers, by
reason of the ground over which they run,
breed larger Trouts.*"*
        —Izaak Walton, *The Compleat Angler*

FROM DENVER, IT'S an easy day trip to most of the destinations presented so far in this book. But of all Front Range waters, none is as renowned and captivating as the South Platte River. Located south of Denver and west of Colorado Springs, the South Platte rates among the country's premiere trout fisheries. Though not as well known, its middle and south forks have excellent fishing too. Whether you explore the main river or its tributaries, you'll discover some wonderful places to fish, a dozen of which are described in this chapter.

The South Platte is the only major tailwater in the Front Range. Tailwaters neither flow freely nor occur naturally; they're engineered—mainly for purposes of irrigation, power generation, and human consumption. Along the South Platte's course, a series of reservoirs impound water, and at the reservoirs' outlets, bottom-release dams discharge regulated amounts of water downstream, back into the river. When well managed, a tailwater can offer superb, year-round fly fishing. South Platte water temperatures remain relatively constant throughout the year, and large sections of the river (notably, those downstream of Spinney Mountain Reservoir) may fish well even in the coldest months of winter. In addition, the South Platte holds dense populations of aquatic insects and other foods that encourage the growth of the river's trout, mainly rainbows and browns.

Much of what the trout eat (such as midges, mayflies, and scuds) is exceptionally small, generally corresponding to hook sizes #28 to #18. Especially during high-water periods, the trout also consume larger foods, such as cranefly larvae, aquatic worms, and other fish. As a rule, though, whatever the season or stretch of water, South Platte trout demonstrate a strong preference for minuscule meals. Some time-tested subsurface flies include the RS-2, Miracle Nymph, Dale's Midge Larva, Brassy, Pheasant Tail, and Hare's Ear, sizes #24 to #18. Among the finest dry flies and emergers are the Blue-Winged Olive (standard or parachute), Comparadun, Adams, Rusty Spinner, Ant, Griffith's Gnat, Befus Parachute Emerger, and Hill's Stillborn Emerger, sizes #26 to #18. From July through mid-October, many of the river's slack waters produce the best trico mayfly spinner falls of the Front Range. The events most often occur between 8 A.M. and noon, and the insects correspond to hook sizes #26 to #20. In the river's upper reaches, flies such as the Colorado King, Herl Nymph, Caddis Larva, and Henryville Special can be effective too, but downstream of Elevenmile Canyon, caddisflies and stoneflies are not as prolific or as desirable to trout as they are in other Front Range waters. Insect emergences within a tailwater often occur at different times of year than they do within freestone streams. See Figure 17 (Seasonal Occurrences of Principal Trout Foods, South Platte River).

Trout aren't the only sizable fish that inhabit the South Platte. Pike, some over 2 feet long, frequent stretches of the river near the Cheesman, Elevenmile, and Spinney Mountain reservoirs. In the autumn, spawning Kokanee salmon, most weighing between 2 and 6 pounds, leave their reservoir homes and venture into the river's flows. However, the large, sly trout receive the greatest fly-angling attention. An 8- to 9-foot rod rated for a 4- or 5-weight line is well adapted to most South Platte fly fishing, though you might fish a 6-weight rod in extremely windy conditions or for casting large, weighted, subsurface flies. Whatever fly rod you choose, its tip should be relatively soft in order to avoid breaking off larger trout. In some areas of the river, trout in the 5- to 10-pound range are not uncommon.

When fishing small dry flies or nymphs in the river's many smooth, flat waters, long (10- to 12-foot) leaders tapered to 6X or 7X and delicate, drag-free presentations will prove productive. So will good measures of experience, patience, and luck.

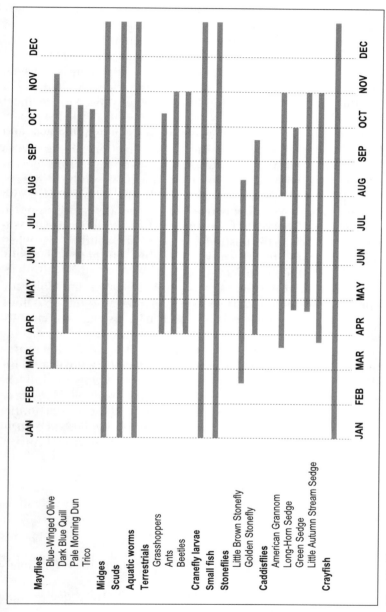

Fig. 18. Seasonal Occurrences of Principal Trout Foods

Even in the least-fished areas, South Platte trout tend to be extraordinarily cautious and easily spooked. In his book *Fly Fishing the South Platte River*, Roger Hill suggests that the South Platte angler wear knee pads and cast from a kneeling position. You can then approach fish more closely, gain far better control over fly presentation, and perhaps most importantly, conceal your presence from the fish. Roger's right; the technique works beautifully. You can buy lightweight nylon kneepads at most hardware stores.

First-time or infrequent visitors to the South Platte should know of a peculiarity regarding the direction of the river's flows. The typical Front Range stream or river runs downstream from west to east, or from north to south. However, from around the town of Lake George to Denver, the South Platte River moves downstream in a generally south-to-north course. Near Cheesman Canyon, for example, downstream waters lie to the north; upstream ones, to the south. Even when they're prepared for it, many anglers find this geographic oddity at least a little disorienting.

Because of the river's proximity to Denver and Colorado Springs, the South Platte receives a fair amount of fishing pressure, mainly on weekends and in areas that are close to roadways. For these reasons, plan your South Platte fishing trips for weekdays and seek destinations that lie off the beaten path. The river's most popular and heavily fished waters are those of Cheesman Canyon, Elevenmile Canyon, and the stretches near the towns of Deckers and Trumbull. However, the South Platte has many more trout-fishing opportunities than these, from around the river's south and middle forks near Alma and Fairplay downstream to Waterton Canyon, just south of Denver.

WATERTON CANYON
(See map page 134.)

Management: USFS; Denver Water Board.

Area maps: USFS map, Pike National Forest; Trails Illustrated Map 135; DeLorme maps 40 and 50.

Elevations: Trailhead: 5,520 feet. Destination: 5,786 feet.

Hiking distance: Up to 5.5 miles.

Hike rating: Easy to difficult, depending upon the distance. If you can, travel by horseback or mountain bike.

Special regulations: From 300 yards north of the Marston Diversion upstream to the Strontia Springs Dam, fishing is restricted to catch-and-release with artificial flies or lures.

Directions: From Denver, take Colorado 121 (South Wadsworth Boulevard) south. About 3.3 miles south of Chatfield State Park, turn left (south) on Waterton Road. Continue another 0.2 mile to the parking area on the left (east) side of the road. The Waterton Canyon Trailhead is located opposite the parking area, on the west side of Waterton Road. Follow the Waterton Canyon Trail along the river.

The canyon trail is actually a graded dirt road nearly two lanes wide, with travel there restricted to "nonmotorized" transportation. Hiking is slow going, but a mountain bike offers a quick, enjoyable way of negotiating the canyon. Riding at a moderate pace, you'll make about 5 or 6 miles an hour on the gradual ascent up the canyon toward the Strontia Springs Dam. The return trip is easier and faster, a nearly continual descent back to the trailhead. The trail runs close by the river, and from your vantage point on a bicycle, you'll have an exceptionally good view of the water.

Along its route, the trail is well marked with signs and mileposts. For the first couple of miles, scrub oak and willow grow along the streambanks and the water moves mostly in 30-foot-wide runs interspersed with riffles and a few deep pools. Fishing there is good, but it gets even better farther up the rocky canyon. The prime waters lie between the Marston Diversion (a dam-like structure located about 3 miles from the trailhead) and the Strontia Springs Dam (about 3 miles upstream of the Marston Diversion).

In the upper reaches, many of the river's browns and rainbows measure well over 14 inches. Boulders are scattered about the rocky and weedy streambed, and the waters flow in runs, riffles, and pockets, as well as in deep pools and long, broad glides. Fish the pocket waters and other fast-moving currents with short-line casts. The slow, flat reaches demand longer, more delicate presentations. Remember to watch out for rattlers. They're common in the canyon, and often sun themselves on or near the trail.

STRONTIA SPRINGS TO DECKERS
(See map page 134.)

Management: USFS; Denver Water Board; private.

Area maps: USFS map, Pike National Forest; Trails Illustrated Map 135; DeLorme maps 40 and 50.

Average elevation: 6,240 feet.

Hiking distance: Most of the river flows within a few hundred yards of the road.

Hike rating: Easy.

Special regulations: From the Strontia Springs Dam upstream to the Scraggy View Picnic Ground, the trout bag and possession limit is two fish. From the Scraggy View Picnic Ground upstream to the lower boundary of the Wigwam Club, fishing is restricted to artificial flies or lures. The trout bag and possession limit is two fish 16 inches or longer. (Founded in 1921, the Wigwam Club is a private fishing club that owns about 2 miles of the South Platte River as well as adjoining lands.)

Directions: From Denver, there are several routes into this general section of the South Platte River. Here are two of them: (1) From Denver, take U.S. 285 south and west. Turn left (south) on County Road 97 (Foxton Road). Turn left (east) on County Road 96 (South Platte River Road), which leads to the settlement of South Platte, at the confluence of the North Fork and main stream of the South Platte River. (2) From Denver, take U.S. 85 south and east. Near Sedalia, turn right (west) on Colorado 67. West of Pine Nook, Colorado 67 becomes County Road 67. Follow County Road 67 south and west. At Sprucewood, you can take County Road 40 west to the river (near Nighthawk, about 5 miles upstream of South Platte). Alternately, stay on County Road 67, which also will take you to the river (near Oxyoke, about 9 miles upstream of South Platte).

Although just one main road parallels the South Platte River from the confluence of the North Fork upstream to Deckers, its name changes along the route. From the confluence upstream to the junction of County Road 67 (about 1.5 miles south and east of the Scraggy View Picnic Ground), the road is named County Road 97. Upstream of the junction, County Road 97 becomes County Road 67.

Though most fly anglers overlook the river's lower reaches, where bait fishing is allowed (downstream of Scraggy View Picnic Ground), the waters still offer plenty of worthwhile fly-fishing opportunities. Just north of the confluence of the North Fork and the main stream of the South Platte River, and within view of the vacant, tumbledown South Platte Hotel, watch for an unmarked parking area on the east side of County Road 96 (South Platte River Road). From the parking area, you can hike an old, unnamed, and nearly level dirt road that follows the South Platte east and north for about 1 mile downstream through a rocky canyon toward the Strontia Springs Reservoir. As you near the reservoir, the water broadens and slows its course, and trout there often rise to small (sizes #24 to #20) imitations of adult or emergent midges and mayflies. South of the confluence, hotel, and parking area, other sections of the river lie within a quick walk of the road, where parking is available in and near numerous picnic and camping areas. Check out the waters near Nighthawk, the Osprey Camping Area, and the Willow Bend Picnic Ground; they hold good-sized browns and rainbows.

Fly anglers prefer the area's upper reaches, where bait fishing is prohibited, from Scraggy View Picnic Ground upstream toward Trumbull and Deckers. There the river flows in glides, runs, and riffles along a gentle gradient, and willows and grasses line the streambanks. Upstream of Deckers, the streambanks become increasingly rocky and steep. County Road 75 (located near the junction of County Road 67 and County Road 126 in Deckers) parallels about 1 mile of the river in the vicinity of the Lone Rock Campground. Additional access to the upper river lies along County Road 126, which heads west and south toward the Gill Trail and the waters of Cheesman Canyon.

CHEESMAN CANYON
(See map page 134.)

Management: USFS; CDOW.

Area maps: USFS map, Pike National Forest; Trails Illustrated Map 135; DeLorme maps 40 and 50.

Average elevation: 6,560 feet.

Hiking distance: 0.8 mile.

Hike rating: Easy to moderate.

Special regulations: From the Wigwam Club upstream to Cheesman dam, fishing is restricted to catch-and-release with artificial flies or lures.

Directions: From Denver, there are two main routes to the Gill Trail and parking area, located about 2.5 miles west and south of the town of Deckers: (1) Take U.S. 285 south and west. Near Pine Junction, turn left (south and east) on County Road 126. South of the Wigwam Campground, continue on County Road 126 as it curves sharply to the left (east). Park at the Gill Trail parking area, which lies on the left (north) side of County Road 126, just east of the road's sharp curve. (2) Take U.S. 85 south and east. Near Sedalia, turn right (west) on Colorado 67. West of Pine Nook, Colorado 67 merges into County Road 67. Follow County Road 67 south and west. Then either take County Road 40 west to County Road 97 or stay on County Road 67; both routes lead to the river. Head south on the main road that parallels the river. At the town of Deckers, bear right (north and west) on County Road 126. Follow County Road 126 about 2.5 miles to the Gill Trail parking area, which lies on the right (north) side of the road.

The Gill Trailhead is on the south side of County Road 126 near the main parking area. The Gill Trail follows the river for a few miles up toward the Cheesman Reservoir Dam.

After you've hiked the Gill Trail for 20 minutes or so, the river will come into view, and it's a spectacular sight. Boulders rise from deep, broad pools, and the water flows between the steep, red-rock walls of the canyon. Hike in a bit farther and you'll see a greater variety of water, including runs and riffles. Gaze into some of the slow-moving waters and you'll likely begin to see trout, and large ones too. Cheesman Canyon trout are some of the biggest—and most difficult to catch—in all the river. Nevertheless, some simple approaches can fool them. In brief: Choose the right fly, use the best presentation, and go fishing in lousy weather.

Some of the canyon's finest fishing opportunities develop on cool, overcast days, or during periods of rain, drizzle, or snow. At these times, blue-winged olive mayflies or midges often emerge in profusion, and the normally wary trout rise freely to feed on them—or on your carefully presented imitation. Even in the absence of a hatch, cloudy skies and foul weather frequently make the trout less skittish and more likely to strike at a fly. Whether you fish dry flies or nymphs, they are best cast up- and across-stream using a leader at least 10 feet long tapered to 6X or finer. In the canyon, nymph fishing tends to be more productive than dry-fly fishing, especially when you fish a section of water thoroughly. The trout seldom need move far, if at all, to eat the abundant natural foods that come their way. For example, a subsurface fly that drifts 4 inches from a trout's nose may not hold any interest for the fish. But should your next presentation move 2 or 3 inches closer to your prey, it may well be time to set the hook and prepare for a fight. When nymph fishing, never hesitate to add, remove, or reposition the weight on your leader in order to attain the best presentation. If you use strike indicators, keep them as small and inconspicuous as practical.

Generally, you can count on just a half-dozen fly patterns that are particularly well suited for fishing Cheesman Canyon. They include the Brassy and RS-2 (gray or olive), sizes #24 to #20, and the Pheasant Tail (natural or olive), sizes #20 to #16. On or near the surface, try the Griffith's Gnat, Blue-Winged Olive, and Parachute Emerger, sizes #24 to #20.

You can reach the canyon's upper waters by driving west and south on Forest Road 211 (near the Gill Trailhead) toward the Cheesman Reservoir Dam and a parking area. Then walk about 1.4 miles south on an unmarked but well-worn trail to the river. Most of this hike is level, but during the last 0.3 mile or so, the trail descends about 300 feet. Fishing the upper waters is wonderful: Few anglers go there, and the trout are not as selective as their downstream cousins. At day's end, these benefits exact their price—a grueling hike back up the hill.

HAPPY MEADOWS
(See map page 134.)

Management: USFS; private.

Area maps: USFS map, Pike National Forest; USGS map, Hackett Mountain; DeLorme maps 61 and 49.

Elevations: Trailhead: 7,670. Destination: 7,613 feet.

Hiking distance: 2 miles.

Hike rating: Moderate.

Special regulations: None.

Directions: From Denver or Colorado Springs, take U.S. 24 west through the town of Lake George. Turn right (north) on County Road 77. Continue about 1.3 miles, then turn right (east) on County Road 112, the entrance to the Happy Meadows Campground. Follow County Road 112 about 2 miles to the Platte River Trailhead parking area, located on the left (north) side of the road. Follow Trail 654 to the river.

Trail 654 follows a relatively gentle course as it crosses the mountainside, its steepest sections lying nearest the river canyon. At a moderate pace, the hike takes about an hour. The stretch of river that you first see flows in smooth, broad glides. A short distance downstream, however, the water breaks into riffles and farther downstream, into deep, bouldered runs, pockets, and plunge pools that lie within a narrower stream channel. My friend Leigh lives in the town of Lake George and has fished these waters since 1959. His observations speak volumes about fly fishing the South Platte River from the Lake George region downstream to Tarryall Creek. He notes that the area is "trophy water, loaded with browns, where dudes hardly ever go. And if you want to catch big fish, don't bother with dry flies or any kind of big flies. Wherever you fish there, use a light-colored midge larva, size #22 or #20. Never go heavier than 5X (6X is better), but use lots of weight to get the fly down fast. And when that fish hits—Hold on!" I've followed his advice. It works. Two fly patterns are especially effective: the Miracle Nymph and Dale's Midge Larva, sizes #22 to #20.

Two other trails (which are more steep and difficult to hike) can also take you into this general vicinity. Both trails are accessed via Forest Road 210, which lies north of the Happy Meadows Campground and east of County Road 77. A roughly 2-mile hike along Trail 619 brings you to the confluence of Tarryall Creek and the South Platte River. Hike about 1 mile on Trail 626 and you'll arrive at a point about midway between Tarryall Creek and the Happy Meadows Campground.

ELEVENMILE CANYON
(See map page 134.)

Management: USFS; private.

Area maps: USFS map, Pike National Forest; USGS map, Elevenmile Canyon; DeLorme map 61.

Average elevation: 8,200 feet.

Hiking distance: Most of the river flows within a few hundred yards of the road.

Hike rating: Easy.

Special regulations: Fishing is restricted to artificial flies or lures. The trout bag and possession limit is two fish of 16 inches or longer.

Directions: From Denver or Colorado Springs, take U.S. 24 west toward the town of Lake George. Turn left (south and west) on County Road 96. Continue about 0.9 mile to the entry station and purchase an area use permit. (In 1997, permit cost was $3 a day.) The road follows the river for about 9 miles.

Easy accessibility and excellent fishing for rainbows and browns make Elevenmile Canyon a favorite destination among Front Range fly anglers. Most of this 9-mile stretch of the South Platte flows just yards away from the road, and several campgrounds and picnic areas are nearby. In some places, the river is bounded by grassy, nearly level banks; in others, by steep canyon walls. Lush beds of aquatic weeds grow upon much of the rocky, uneven streambed, parts of which are silted and slippery. Be careful wading there. The river averages about 40 feet wide and flows in varied types of waters, from long, slow-moving glides and runs to sparkling riffles, pockets, and plunge pools. During times of low to moderate flows, the river becomes remarkably clear. From a vantage point along the road or streambank, take the time to look into the water and locate where trout might be holding or feeding. At any time of year, scuds (tan or yellow-orange, sizes #18 to #14) rate among the most productive flies in Elevenmile Canyon. In fast or deep waters, a purple Woolly Bugger (sizes #10 to #6) or San Juan Worm (tan or red, sizes #14 to #10) can be effective too. During the summer and fall, ants and beetles (sizes #22 to #18) serve as some of the best dry flies, especially when presented near the shorelines.

A Quick Look at South Park

Upstream of Elevenmile Canyon and Elevenmile Reservoir, the South Platte River meanders through vast expanses of high prairie in a region known as South Park, in Park County. The rocky canyons that typify the river's downstream reaches drop from view, and the water flows through extraordinary, flat, exposed grasslands flanked by small, rolling hills and distant mountain peaks. For many of the creatures (including trout) that live there, this wide-open and mostly treeless terrain offers little protection from the area's many predators, such as blue herons, eagles, hawks, owls, foxes, coyotes, and humans. Only the most wary and vigilant of potential prey escape them. In large part, successful fly fishing in such an inherently perilous environment depends upon the angler's stealth. Keep low to the bank or streambed when casting, and minimize false-casting. When fishing from shore or hiking along it, walk softly, staying several feet away from the banks. When wading, don't drag your feet along the streambed, but raise them with every step to keep from disturbing the water and to minimize noise. Wear subdued colors and avoid allowing your shadow to fall upon the sections of water you plan to fish. Take advantage of weather conditions, such as rain, snow, or overcast skies, that can help mask your presence. When possible, during periods of intermittent breezes or winds, cast while the breeze or wind is blowing and ruffling the water's surface, not after the air and water have become calm. (In South Park, you seldom need wait long for the wind to blow.) Watch your step as you walk through the grasslands; they conceal numerous holes excavated by badgers and prairie dogs.

The southern two-thirds of Park County, which is home to many prime South Platte fly-fishing destinations, is sparsely populated and services are few. Just several hundred people live in the county seat, Fairplay, located at the junction of U.S. 285 and Colorado 9. Fairplay, a friendly and picturesque old mining town, has a few restaurants and motels, a couple of gas stations, and a general store. The tiny village of Hartsel lies about 18 miles to the south, near the intersection of U.S. 24 and Colorado 9. By the way, in 1972 an angler fishing the South Platte River within Park County landed a 32-inch, nearly 18.5-pound rainbow trout and so established a Colorado state fishing record that stands today. I'm told that in recent years, some fly anglers have caught, measured, and weighed even larger rainbows in the South Platte River, but then revived the fish and released them back into the amazing waters from which they came. With luck, you'll have the opportunity to do the same.

SPINNEY MOUNTAIN RANCH STATE WILDLIFE AREA DOWNSTREAM OF SPINNEY MOUNTAIN RESERVOIR
(See map page 134.)

Management: USFS; CDOW.

Area maps: USFS map, Pike National Forest; CDOW map, Spinney Mountain Ranch State Wildlife Area; DeLorme maps 48, 49, and 61.

Average elevation: 8,700 feet.

Hiking distance: The river lies a few hundred yards from the parking area.

Hike rating: Easy.

Special regulations: Fishing is restricted to catch-and-release with artificial flies or lures.

Directions: From Hartsel, take County Road 59 (near the junction of U.S. 24 and Colorado 9) east about 12.9 miles. Near the road's junction with County Road 447 (High Chaparral Road) to the north, County Road 59 turns sharply to the right (south). Follow County Road 59 about 1 mile to a parking area.

Characterized by sharp bends, long glides, deep runs, riffles, and grassy, undercut banks, this section of the South Platte averages about 50 feet wide and holds some of the river's largest trout, mainly rainbows and cutts. Trout 20 inches or longer are common; in early autumn, good-sized brown trout move into this stretch of water during their spawning runs. The standard complement of South Platte flies work well here, but in periods of moderate to high flows, try deep-drifting a size #1/0 or #2/0 rusty-orange crayfish pattern. The long-horn sedge, its wings and body about the same color as the dried grasses found along the shoreline, emerges in fair numbers from May through the end of September, and is well imitated by a ginger-hackled, size #16 Henryville Special. The streambed is composed variously of small rocks, gravel, sand, and silt. Aquatic weeds are common and help nurture substantial populations of scuds. The transitional or "seam" areas between differing types of water (such as riffles and runs) can prove some of the most productive areas to fish, as can the undercut banks and deep pools. In most years, this is the westernmost section of the South Platte River that remains relatively ice-free throughout the winter, when dead-drifting small, subsurface midge or mayfly imitations often yields the best results.

SPINNEY MOUNTAIN RANCH STATE WILDLIFE AREA UPSTREAM OF SPINNEY MOUNTAIN RESERVOIR
(See map page 134.)

Management: USFS; CDOW.

Area maps: USFS map, Pike National Forest; CDOW map, Spinney Mountain Ranch State Wildlife Area; DeLorme maps 48, 49, and 61.

Average elevation: 8,800 feet.

Hiking distance: 0.3 mile.

Hike rating: Easy.

Special regulations: Fishing is restricted to artificial flies or lures. All trout between 12 and 20 inches long must be released. The trout bag and possession limit is two fish, only one of which may be longer than 20 inches.

Directions: From Hartsel, take County Road 59 (near the junction of U.S. 24 and Colorado 9) east about 3.5 miles. Park in the parking area located on the right (south) side of the road near several vacant, old ranch buildings.

Though this isn't the only access point for the upper sections of the Spinney Mountain Ranch State Wildlife Area, the historic old ranch site, with its rustic homestead, barns, corrals, and outbuildings, is a favorite of many anglers. Both the scenery and the fishing are superb. To reach the river, walk about 10 minutes due south across the meadow, sections of which are strewn with the sun-bleached bones of cattle. This stretch of the South Platte is similar in character to the winding waters downstream of Spinney Mountain Reservoir, but a bit smaller, usually running between 30 and 40 feet wide. In addition, the stream bottom isn't as weedy, though more willows and shrubs grow along the shoreline. As you stand in the river and face upstream, you have a marvelous view of mountain peaks that spread across nearly all of the western horizon. In addition to midge patterns, various life-stage imitations of blue-winged olives (sizes #22 to #16) and pale morning duns (sizes #18 to #16) are among the best flies to use here. From mid-summer through late September, the grassy meadows adjoining the streambanks abound with grasshoppers, sizes #12 to #8, most of them yellow, tan, or olive in color. In the river's many smooth-flowing glides, low-floating, parachute-style hopper patterns work best.

BADGER BASIN STATE WILDLIFE AREA, MIDDLE FORK
(See map page 134.)

Management: CDOW.

Area maps: USFS map, Pike National Forest; CDOW map, Badger Basin State Wildlife Area; DeLorme maps 48, 49, and 60.

Average elevation: 8,900 feet.

Hiking distance: The river flows within a few hundred yards of the parking areas.

Hike rating: Easy.

Special regulations: Fishing is restricted to artificial flies or lures. All trout between 12 and 20 inches long must be released. The trout bag and possession limit is two fish, only one of which may be longer than 20 inches.

Directions: The Middle Fork of the South Platte River flows through two sections of the Badger Basin State Wildlife Area (where parking places may or may not be marked with signs). *To the lower section:* From Hartsel, take U.S. 24 east about 2 miles. Turn right (south) on Nelson Platte Ranch Road. Continue about 0.5 mile to a parking area. *To the upper section:* Follow County Road 439 (located off U.S. 24 in the center of Hartsel) north about 1.3 miles to a parking area.

The lower and upper sections of this State Wildlife Area are similar, but the upper section (accessed via County Road 439) merits the most attention if only because it offers a larger

expanse of water to fish. Much of the land and some of the
water in Badger Basin shows the effects of years of overgrazing
by cattle. An overabundance of silt is present in some of the
streambed, and apart from grasses, the highest-growing vegetation you'll find is an occasional, scrawny willow. As the Colorado Division of Wildlife and other organizations and
individuals work to restore this area, it will likely become a far
more beautiful and popular fishing destination. Today, however, most fly anglers avoid Badger Basin. The place lacks much
of the aesthetic appeal of other, nearby fishing areas. In addition, fishing in Badger Basin is often a challenging (and sometimes discouraging) experience.

Regardless, the river holds large numbers of trout, especially browns and a scattering of rainbows, many of which are
well-fed and over a foot long. Prominent insect life there includes
blue-winged olives, pale morning duns, and midges. American
grannoms populate the water as well. Within Badger Basin, the
Middle Fork of the South Platte River is from 25 to 30 feet wide
and flows mostly in glides; riffles are relatively few. There are also
small, deep, silt-bottomed pools that provide good holding areas
for the river's wary trout. Generally, though, the prime fish-hid-
ing places are the water's numerous undercut banks. Try presenting large grasshopper patterns (sizes #12 to #10) or small
dry-fly ants or beetles (sizes #18 to #22) tight to the streambanks.
A subsurface double-fly rig cast down- and across-stream so that
it swings up close to the shore can be effective too. Use a size #16
Partridge-and-Orange as a point fly and, tied about a foot below
it, a size #20 or #22 Brassy or other midge-type fly. For the de-
voted fly angler, Badger Basin is worth the trip.

TOMAHAWK AND BUFFALO PEAKS STATE WILDLIFE AREAS, MIDDLE FORK
(See map page 134.)

Management: CDOW.

Area maps: USFS map, Pike National Forest; CDOW map: Buffalo Peaks, Knight-Imler, and Tomahawk State Wildlife Areas;
DeLorme map 48.

Average elevation: 9,000 feet.

Hiking distance: The river flows within a few hundred yards of
the parking areas.

Hike rating: Easy.

Special regulations: In the Knight-Imler and Buffalo Peaks State Wildlife Areas, public access is prohibited beyond 25 feet from the stream's center. Fishing is restricted to artificial flies or lures. All trout between 12 and 20 inches long must be released. The trout bag and possession limit is two fish, only one of which may be longer than 20 inches.

Directions: To the Tomahawk State Wildlife Area, lower reaches: From Hartsel, take Colorado 9 north about 4.8 miles, then turn right (east) onto a dirt road marked by a state wildlife area sign. Follow the dirt road 1 mile to a parking area. *To the Tomahawk State Wildlife Area, upper reaches:* From Hartsel, take Colorado 9 north about 7 miles, then turn right (east) onto a dirt road marked by a state wildlife area sign. Follow the dirt road about 1.9 miles to a closed gate. Open the gate, drive through, and then close the gate behind you. Continue another 0.1 mile and cross a small wooden bridge to reach the parking area.

To the Buffalo Peaks State Wildlife Area: From Hartsel, take Colorado 9 north about 7.2 miles (just north of the settlement of Garo). There the river flows to the west of the highway and within the Buffalo Peaks State Wildlife Area. The Buffalo Peaks State Wildlife Area adjoins the northern boundary of the Tomahawk State Wildlife Area and can also be reached by hiking or wading in from Tomahawk's upper reaches.

The lands and waters of these two Colorado state wildlife areas are wonderfully vibrant. In places, streamside vegetation is dense and overhangs the river, providing shelter and food for numerous brown, rainbow, and cutthroat trout. The winding, largely rock-and-gravel-bottomed water teems with the cased larvae of American grannoms as well as blue-winged olives and midges. Riffles, runs, pockets, and glides flow around the tiny islands and bits of deadfall that dot the river's course. The work of beavers is evident, with much of the river flowing off into small side channels where some of the larger trout feed and conceal themselves. The streambed varies in width from about 15 to 25 feet across. You'll see that nearly every section of the river seems a likely spot to catch trout. Try presenting a Hill's Stillborn Emerger, sizes #22 to #20, on or slightly beneath the water's surface. The Herl Nymph and Prince Nymph, sizes #18 to #14, are good choices for subsurface patterns. A purple Zonker, sizes #10 to #6, is a favorite streamer, best fished down-and-across and then retrieved either rapidly or slowly. In the midst of the area's great fishing, remember to take some time to savor the spectacular views of the mountains to the south.

ALMA STATE WILDLIFE AREA, MIDDLE FORK
(See map page 134.)

Management: CDOW.

Area maps: USFS map, Pike National Forest; CDOW map, Alma State Wildlife Area; DeLorme map 48.

Average elevation: 10,400 feet.

Hiking distance: The river flows within a few hundred yards of the parking area.

Hike rating: Easy.

Special regulations: Fishing is restricted to artificial flies or lures. All trout between 12 and 20 inches long must be released. The trout bag and possession limit is two fish, only one of which may be longer than 20 inches.

Directions: From Hartsel, take Colorado 9 north about 22.5 miles through Fairplay to the center of Alma. Follow Colorado 9 north about 1.1 miles through Alma to County Road 4. Drive another 0.1 mile to the parking area located on the left (west) side of County Road 4.

The Alma State Wildlife Area is located in a valley about 5.5 miles southeast of the Continental Divide and within view of several mountains that exceed 13,000 feet in elevation. Here the Middle Fork of the South Platte River is only about 15 to 20 feet wide, its twisted, intertwining waters often flowing through side channels and wetlands. Upstream of the parking area, there are several beaver dams and fair-sized, silty-bottomed ponds. The trout include browns, brookies, and rainbows, most of them between 9 and 13 inches long. In the moving waters, the Deerhair Caddis, Stimulator, Adams, and Henryville Special, sizes #18 to #12, are among the most productive dry flies. Dry-fly and emerger midge patterns are effective in the ponds, as are subsurface patterns such as the Wet Cahill and Grizzly-and-Orange, sizes #18 to #14. Gravel and small stones cover most of the streambed, and a healthy population of small trees, shrubs, and other vegetation lines the streambanks. Despite the relatively small size of the river, there's still plenty of room to cast an 8- or 8.5-foot rod. Although this section of the river is ideally suited to a 2- or 3-weight rod, you'll likely need to use a 4- or 5-weight model just to contend with frequent and predominantly downslope winds. Because the Alma State Wildlife Area is a popular destination for summer tourists, it's usually best to make your trips there before Independence Day and after Labor Day.

BADGER BASIN STATE WILDLIFE AREA, SOUTH FORK
(See map page 134.)

Management: CDOW.

Area maps: USFS map, Pike National Forest; CDOW map, Badger Basin State Wildlife Area; DeLorme map 48.

Average elevation: 8,800 feet.

Hiking distance: Much of the river flows within a few hundred yards of a road or parking area.

Hike rating: Easy.

Special regulations: Fishing is restricted to artificial flies or lures. All trout between 12 and 20 inches long must be released. The trout bag and possession limit is two fish, only one of which may be longer than 20 inches. However, on the South Fork of the South Platte River above the Colorado 9 bridge and upstream toward Antero Reservoir, bait fishing is permitted. There the trout bag and possession limit is four fish, regardless of size.

Directions: The South Fork of the South Platte River flows through two sections of the Badger Basin State Wildlife Area. *To the lower section (which adjoins the western boundary of the Spinney Mountain Ranch State Wildlife Area):* From Hartsel, take County Road 59 southeast about 0.7 mile to a parking area. *To the upper section (which lies east of the Antero Reservoir State Wildlife Area):* The upper section of Badger Basin is located west of Hartsel along U.S. 24 and within view of the highway.

A few years ago, I stood on the banks of the South Fork in Badger Basin and spoke with a field officer of the Colorado Division of Wildlife. We discussed the eroded streambanks (caused by overgrazing) and the food-rich streambed. I asked why he thought so few people fished the river there. "Because the novice anglers get so frustrated," he said. "But the more experienced ones can get some pretty decent fish." "Pretty decent fish" seems a polite understatement. This roughly 25- to 30-foot-wide stretch of river holds many large browns and a few rainbows as well. However, they're easy to spook and difficult to catch. As in the Middle Fork of the South Platte River in the same state wildlife area, South Fork trout generally keep close to or beneath undercut banks. In the South Fork's many flat, slow-moving waters, using a 12-foot leader tapered to 6X or 7X will likely be helpful. Scud imitations (either size #18 and tan or size #14 and yellow-orange) rate among the most productive fly patterns.

Parts of Badger Basin and other state wildlife areas in the region include grasslands where buffalo are pastured. It might seem romantic to be fly casting within sight of these great creatures grazing on the high prairie; but be forewarned that their actions are highly unpredictable and potentially dangerous. Because most state wildlife areas are securely fenced and offer few openings along their fencelines, and because you and the buffalo might well be sharing the same enclosed pasture, it's always wise to keep some distance between you and your livestock companions.

KNIGHT-IMLER AND 63 RANCH STATE WILDLIFE AREAS, SOUTH FORK
(See map page 134.)

Management: CDOW.

Area maps: USFS map, Pike National Forest; CDOW map, Buffalo Peaks, Knight-Imler, and Tomahawk state wildlife areas; CDOW map, Antero Reservoir and 63 Ranch state wildlife areas; DeLorme maps 48 and 60.

Average elevation: 9,000 feet.

Hiking distance: The river flows within a few hundred yards of the parking areas.

Hike rating: Easy.

Special regulations: Fishing is restricted to artificial flies or lures. All trout between 12 and 20 inches long must be released.

The trout bag and possession limit is two fish, only one of which may be longer than 20 inches.

Directions: To the Knight-Imler State Wildlife Area: From Fairplay, take U.S. 285 south about 11.2 miles to a parking area located on the left (east) side of the road. *To the 63 Ranch State Wildlife Area:* From Fairplay, follow U.S. 285 south about 14.2 miles to a parking area located on the left (east) side of the road.

Within Knight-Imler, the South Fork runs only about 20 feet across and teems with smaller (9- to 13-inch) brown trout. Most of the water flows in glides and riffles, with occasional deep holes located near the river's bends; a light layer of silt covers much of the rocky streambed, but without any apparent harm to the river's aquatic life. American grannoms flourish there, as do midges, scuds, and blue-winged olives. A Parachute Adams, sizes #20 to #16, works well as a dry fly. A Herl Nymph, sizes #14 to #12, is effective subsurface, along with scud imitations, sizes #18 to #14. Wading is seldom necessary. When fishing, keep low to the banks and about 5 feet or so away from them. The grassy streamside offers no place of concealment for the fly angler, and the fish are easily spooked by movements onshore or by shadows on the water.

At the 63 Ranch (about 3 miles downstream and south of Knight-Imler), the streambed takes on a more winding, narrow course. The trout there are generally larger than they are at Knight-Imler, often reaching a length of 16 inches or more. Parts of the river are reminiscent of a zigzagging marshland creek. At nearly every bend, the water deepens, forming retreats and feeding areas for the river's many brown trout. The banks hold large numbers of ants and grasshoppers, in addition to some well-hidden strands of rusty barbed wire. Morning and evening spinner falls of blue-winged olives (sizes #20 to #16) stimulate surface feeding among the usually cautious trout. An orange scud (size #18 or #16) with a Miracle Nymph dropper (size #22 or #20) works well subsurface.

APPENDIX: FRONT RANGE
FLY-FISHING RESOURCE GUIDE

State and Federal Land Management Agencies

Colorado Division of Wildlife
6060 Broadway
Denver, CO 80216
(303) 291-7230

U.S. Forest Service, Rocky Mountain Regional Office
740 Simms
Denver, CO 80228
(303) 275-5350

Arapaho and Roosevelt National Forests
240 W. Prospect Rd.
Fort Collins, CO 80526
(970) 498-1100

Pike National Forest
1920 Valley Drive
Pueblo, CO 81008
(719) 545-8737

Rocky Mountain National Park
Estes Park, CO 80517
(970) 586-1206

Bureau of Land Management
2850 Youngfield St.
Lakewood, CO 80215
(303) 239-3600

Arapaho and Roosevelt National Forests District Offices:

Boulder Ranger District
2995 Baseline Rd.
Boulder, CO 80303
(303) 444-6600

Clear Creek Ranger District
101 Chicago Creek
P.O. Box 3307
Idaho Springs, CO 80452
(303) 567-2901

Estes–Poudre Ranger District and Redfeather Ranger District
1311 S. College Ave.
Fort Collins, CO 80524
(970) 498-2775

Pike National Forest District Offices:

Pikes Peak Ranger District
601 S. Weber St.
Colorado Springs, CO 80903
(719) 636-1602

South Park Ranger District
P.O. Box 219
Fairplay, CO 80440
(719) 836-2031

South Platte Ranger District
11177 W. 8th Ave.
Box 25127
Lakewood, CO 80225
(303) 236-5371

County Government Offices

Boulder County
2040 14th St.
Boulder, CO 80302
(303) 441-3131

Clear Creek County
405 Argentine St.
Georgetown, CO 80444
(303) 534-5777

Douglas County
101 Third St.
Castle Rock, CO 80104
(303) 660-7400

Jefferson County
100 Jefferson County Parkway
Golden, CO 80419
(303) 279-6511

Larimer County
200 W. Oak St.
Fort Collins, CO 80521
(970) 498-7000

Park County
501 Main St.
Fairplay, CO 80440
(303) 838-4280

Teller County
101 W. Bennett
Box 959
Cripple Creek, CO 80813
(719) 687-5242

City Government and Agency Offices

Boulder, City of
P.O. Box 791
Boulder, CO 80306
(303) 441-3131

Denver Water Board
1600 W. Twelfth Ave.
Denver, CO 80204
(303) 628-6000

Longmont, City of
350 Kimbark
Longmont, CO 80501
(303) 651-8376

Loveland, City of
500 E. 3rd St.
Loveland, CO 80537
(970) 962-2000

Selected Front Range Fly Shops

Fort Collins–Loveland Area:

Bennett's
121 Bunyan Ave.
Berthoud, CO 80503
(970) 532-2213

Bob's Fly-Tying Specialties
406 S. Lincoln Ave.
Loveland, CO 80537
(970) 667-1107

Butte House Fly Shoppe
4412 W. Eisenhower Blvd.
Loveland, CO 80537
(970) 667-9772

Colorado Wilderness Sports
358 E. Elkhorn Ave.
Estes Park, CO 80517
(970) 586-6548

Selected Front Range Fly Shops
(*continued*)

Estes Angler
338 W. Riverside Dr.
Estes Park, CO 80517
(970) 586-2110

Rocky Mountain Fly Shop
124 E. Monroe Dr.
Fort Collins, CO 80525
(970) 221-9110

St. Peter's Fly Shop
202 Remington St.
Fort Collins, CO 80524
(970) 498-8968

*Longmont–Boulder–
Denver Area:*

Anglers All
5211 S. Santa Fe Dr.
Littleton, CO 80120
(303) 794-1104

Blue Quill Angler
1532 Highway 74
Evergreen, CO 80437
(303) 674-4700

The Bucking Brown Trout Co.
26 E. 1st St.
Nederland, CO 80466
(303) 258-3225

Colorado Angler
1457 Nelson St.
Lakewood, CO 80215
(303) 232-8298

Complete Angler
8547 E. Arapahoe Rd.
Englewood, CO 80112
(303) 694-2387

Denver Angler
5455 W. 38th Ave.
Denver, CO 80212
(303) 403-4512

Duck Creek Sporting Goods
400 S. Boulder Rd.
Lafayette, CO 80026
(303) 665-8845

The Flyfisher, Ltd.
120 Madison St.
Denver, CO 80206
(303) 322-5014

Front Range Anglers
629 S. Broadway
Boulder, CO 80303
(303) 494-1375

Kinsley Outfitters
1155 Thirteenth St.
Boulder, CO 80302
(303) 442-6204

McGuckin Hardware
2525 Arapahoe Ave.
Boulder, CO 80302
(303) 443-1822

Plum Creek Anglers
981 N. Park St.
Castle Rock, CO 80104
(303) 814-0868

River and Stream Co.
8501 W. Bowles Ave.
Littleton, CO 80123
(303) 979-7264

Royal Stevens Ltd.
1610 E. Girard Place
Englewood, CO 80110
(303) 788-0433

St. Vrain Angler
418 Main St.
Longmont, CO 80501
(303) 651-6061

St. Vrain Angler
8951 Harlan St.
Westminster, CO 80030
(303) 412-1111

South Creek, Ltd.
415 Main St.
Lyons, CO 80540
(303) 823-6402

The Trout Fisher
2020 S. Parker Rd.
Denver, CO 80231
(303) 369-7970

Trout's Flyfishing
1069 S. Gaylord St.
Denver, CO 80209
(303) 733-1434

Two Guys Fly Shop
100 E. Cleveland St.
Lafayette, CO 80026
(303) 666-7866

Uncle Milty's Tackle Box
4811 S. Broadway
Englewood, CO 80110
(303) 789-3775

Colorado Springs Area:

Angler's Covey
917 W. Colorado Ave.
Colorado Springs, CO 80905
(719) 471-2984

C/S Angler
3314 Austin Bluffs Parkway
Colorado Springs, CO 80918
(719) 531-5413

General Fishing Tackle
3201 N. El Paso St.
Colorado Springs, CO 80907
(719) 634-6831

Peak Fly Shop
5666 N. Academy Blvd.
Colorado Springs, CO 80918
(719) 260-1415

Pikes Peak Angler
119 N. Tejon St.
Colorado Springs, CO 80903
(719) 636-3348

Tricos
535 Lionstone Dr.
Colorado Springs, CO 80916
(719) 574-5480

Recorded Information

Colorado Department
of Transportation
(Road Conditions)
Recorded information:
(303) 639-1111

Water Talk
(Stream flow information)
(303) 831-7135
Use a touch-tone phone to call.
Once you've made the connec-
tion, press 1*, then the appropriate gauging-station number
followed by *. The following
list includes only selected Water
Talk gauging stations along the
Front Range.

6	South Boulder Creek below Gross Reservoir
7	South Boulder Creek near Eldorado Springs
8	Boulder Creek at Boulder

Recorded Information
(*continued*)

9 Boulder Creek at Orodell
10 Big Thompson River above Lake Estes
11 Big Thompson River below Lake Estes
12 North Fork of the Big Thompson River near Drake
13 Big Thompson River at mouth of canyon
18 Cache la Poudre River at Fort Collins
19 Cache la Poudre River at mouth of canyon
22 Clear Creek near Golden
23 Clear Creek near Lawson
40 South Platte River below Cheesman Reservoir
43 South Platte River above Elevenmile Reservoir
49 South Platte River at Spinney Reservoir

50 South Platte River at South Platte
51 South Platte River below Strontia Springs
52 South Platte River at Waterton
53 South Platte River near Weldonia
56 South Fork of the South Platte River above Antero Reservoir
58 St. Vrain Creek at Lyons

Internet Sites

Two useful fly-fishing Web sites are:

www.flyshop.com/ and
www.streamside.com/

Many other fly-fishing sites exist, but Internet addresses often change. Set your search engine to query on the words "Colorado fly fishing," then bookmark the sites and links you find most helpful.

BIBLIOGRAPHY

Bergman, Ray. *Trout.* New York: Alfred A. Knopf, 1949.

Engle, Ed. *Fly Fishing the Tailwaters.* Harrisburg, Penn.: Stackpole Books, 1991.

Harvey, George. *Techniques of Trout Fishing and Fly Tying.* New York: Lyons and Burford, 1990.

Hill, Roger. *Fly Fishing the South Platte River.* Boulder, Colo.: Pruett Publishing Company, 1991.

Hosman, Todd. *Fly Fishing Rocky Mountain National Park.* Boulder, Colo.: Pruett Publishing Company, 1996.

LaFontaine, Gary. *Caddisflies.* New York: Lyons and Burford, 1981.

Leiser, Eric, and Robert H. Boyle. *Stoneflies for the Angler.* Harrisburg, Penn.: Stackpole Books, 1990.

McCafferty, W. Patrick. *Aquatic Entomology.* Boston: Jones and Bartlett, 1983.

Swisher, Doug, and Carl Richards. *Selective Trout.* New York: Crown, 1971.

Ward, J. V., and B. C. Kondratieff. *An Illustrated Guide to the Mountain Stream Insects of Colorado.* Niwot, Colo.: University Press of Colorado, 1992.

INDEX

Adams, 69; described, 47; using, 126, 136, 152. *See also* Parachute Adams
Alma State Wildlife Area, fishing at, 152–53
Altitude, concerns about, 7–8
American grannoms (*Brachycentrus* sp.): described, 32, 33; using, 89, 109, 151
American Pheasant Tail (PT), described, 60, 61
Anglers All, 158
Angler's Covey, 159
Angling etiquette, 18
Ants, 82; described, 67–68; using, 4, 110, 115, 121, 131, 136, 145, 150, 155
Arapaho National Forest, 75, 156

Backpacks, loading, 12
Badger Basin State Wildlife Area, fishing at, 149–50, 153–54
Bag limit, described, 16
Bard Creek, 129; fishing at, 132–33
Bashline, Jim, 68
Bears, attacks by, 8–9
Beaver Creek, fishing at, 89–91
Beetles: described, 67–68; using, 115, 131, 145, 150
Befus, Brad, 46
Befus Parachute Emergers: described, 46; using, 136
Behavioral drift, 41
Bennett's, 157
Big gray spotted sedge (*Arctopsyche grandis*), described, 34
Big Thompson River, fishing at, 105–6, 107–8, 111–12
Black Gnat, using, 87
BLM. *See* Bureau of Land Management
Blue Lake, fishing at, 120–21
Blue Quill Angler, 158
Blue-winged olives (*Baetis* sp.), 45, 54; described, 40–41, 47, 48, 57; using, 2, 87, 99, 103, 105, 106, 108, 109, 110, 112, 114. *See also* Parachute Blue-Winged Olives
Bob's Fly-Tying Specialties, 157
Brainard Lake, fishing at, 115, 117
Brassy, 34; described, 53; using, 103, 121, 136, 143, 150
Brassy Emergers, described, 54–55
Brook trout: fishing for, 85, 86, 89, 92, 93, 98, 103, 105, 106, 112; introduction of, 13; physical characteristics of, 13–14
Brooks, Charlie, 34
Brown checkered summer sedge (*Polycentropus* sp.), described, 35
Brown drake (*Ameletus* sp.), described, 49
Brown trout: fishing for, 85, 86, 89, 92, 93, 97, 98, 99, 103, 105, 106, 108, 110, 112; introduction of, 13; physical characteristics of, 13–14
Bucking Brown Trout Co., The, 158
Buffalo Peaks State Wildlife Area, fishing at, 150–52
Bureau of Land Management (BLM), 75, 130, 156
Butte House Fly Shoppe, 157

Cache la Poudre River, 77, 78; fishing at, 79–81; North Fork, fishing at, 92, 93–94, 97, 98–99; South Fork, fishing at, 88–89
Caddis case, clues of, 24–25
Caddisflies, 24–35, 22 (fig.), 23 (fig.); adult forms of, 21; egg laying by, 29; emergence of, 28, 29; imitations of, 25–34; life stages of, 25–34; net-spinning, 24, 25; notes on, 32–34; saddle-case, 24, 25; subsurface adult, 28–31; surface, 30–31; tube case, 24; using, 2, 87, 92, 99, 101, 109, 115, 120, 130, 132, 136
Caddis larva, 24; described, 26–27; using, 79, 81, 82, 107, 112, 126, 136
Caddis pupa, described, 27–28
Cahills, 69; described, 47; medium-olive, 133; wet, 29–30, 44–45, 152
Catch-and-release fishing: hatchery trout and, 16; techniques for, 17–18
Caterpillars, 68
CDOW. *See* Colorado Division of Wildlife
Chartreuse Trudes, using, 133
Cheesman Canyon, 138; fishing at, 141–43
Chironomids. *See* Midges
Chung, Rim: RS-2 by, 41
Clear Creek: Bakerville, fishing at, 131–32; Idaho Springs, fishing at, 129–30; South Fork, fishing at, 130–31
Clinger Nymphs, described, 41–42
Clothing, thoughts on, 6–7
Colorado Angler, 158
Colorado Atlas and Gazetteer (DeLorme Mapping), 74
Colorado Department of Transportation, 73, 159
Colorado Division of Water Resources, 73
Colorado Division of Wildlife (CDOW), 9, 78, 150, 156; information from, 7, 16; land management by, 74; maps by, 74
Colorado Fishing Season Information & Wildlife Property Directory, 16
Colorado Kings, 34, 61–62; described, 30–31; using, 90, 94, 113, 117, 136
Colorado River cutthroats, 13
Colorado State Parks, 75
Colorado Wilderness Sports, 157

Parachute Adams: described, 57; using, 80, 87, 155
Parachute Blue-Winged Olives, using, 85
Parachute Emergers, 52, 54; described, 44; using, 87, 114, 115, 118, 119, 121, 127, 136, 143. *See also* Befus Parachute Emergers Parachute Hoppers: described, 65, 67; using, 89
Partridge-and-Grizzly, 67
Partridge-and-Orange, 80; described, 27–28, 44; using, 94, 114, 150
Parvin Lake, fishing at, 96–97
Peak Fly Shop, 159
Pheasant Tail, 43, 67; described, 41; using, 85, 110, 136, 143. *See also* American Pheasant Tail
Pike, 14
Pike National Forest, 75, 156
Pikes Peak Angler, 159
Pliny the Younger, quote of, 73
Plum Creek Anglers, 158
Presentation techniques, 2
Prince, Doug, 61
Prince Nymphs, 52, 61; using, 81, 87, 89, 102, 110, 113, 151
Printer's loupe, using, 20
Private waters, fishing in, 17
PT. *See* American Pheasant Tail

Quill-Body Spinners, described, 47–48
Quill gordons (*Epeorus* sp.), 19, 41, 50; described, 47, 48; using, 79, 99, 124, 127, 132

Rainbow Lakes, fishing at, 122–23
Rainbow trout: fishing for, 89, 92, 93, 97, 98, 99, 103, 105, 106, 108, 110, 112; introduction of, 13; physical characteristics of, 13–14; WD and, 15
Rainstorms, thoughts on, 6
Red quills (*Rhithrogena* sp.), 20, 41; described, 48; using, 79, 81, 94, 99, 105, 107, 109, 112, 127, 132
Reels, 9–12
Regulations, 16–17
Renegade Gnat, using, 87
Rio Grande cutthroats, 13
Rio Grande King, 31
River and Stream Co., 158
Roaring Creek, fishing at, 91
Roaring Creek greenbacks, 91
Roaring River, fishing at, 112–13
Rocky Mountain Fly Shop, 158
Rocky Mountain National Park, 75, 156; fishing at, 110–11
Rocky Mountain whitefish, 14; fishing for, 80, 83
Rods, 9–12
Roll-casting, 10
Roosevelt National Forest, 75, 77, 115, 156
Royal Stevens Ltd., 158
Royal Wulff, 47; using, 81, 106
RS-2, 46; described, 41, 44; using, 136, 143
Rubber Band Nymph: described, 26–27; using, 94, 112

Runoff, fishing during, 4
Rusty Spinners: described, 47–48; using, 110, 127, 136

Saddle-case caddis, 25; described, 24
Safety precautions, 6–9
St. Peter's Fly Shop, 158
St. Vrain Angler, 158, 159
San Juan Worms: described, 68; using, 145
Scuds, 135; described, 70; using, 87, 96, 145, 154, 155
Sedges: big gray, 34; brown checkered summer, 35; giant orange, 35; green, 34, 99, 102, 105, 130; little autumn stream, 33, 109; little black, 35; little plain brown, 34; little spotted, 33, 105; long-horn, 34; pale western stream, 34; short-horn, 33, 130; spotted, 34; summer flyer, 34–35; tan short-horn, 33
Sheep Creek, fishing at, 92–93
Short-horn sedges: described, 33; using, 130
Shucks, 40
63 Ranch State Wildlife Area, fishing at, 154–55
Slate-winged olives (*Drunella coloradensis*), 42; described, 48; using, 120
Snails, described, 70
Sofa Pillows, 35, 61–62; described, 63; using, 113
South Boulder Creek, fishing at, 126–27
South Creek, Ltd., 159
South Park, fishing at, 146–47
South Platte River: fishing at, 135–36; trout foods in, 137
South St. Vrain Creek, fishing at, 101–103, 117–20
Spawning, coloration/shape changes and, 13
Speckled quills (*Callibaetis* sp.), described, 40, 48
Spent adult caddis, described, 32
Spent Damsels, using, 70
Spent Partridge Caddis, 34, 61; using, 87
Spinney Mountain Ranch State Wildlife Area, fishing at 147–49
Splake, 14
Spotted sedge (*Hydropsyche* sp.), described, 34
Stillborn Emergers, using, 115
Stimulators, 52; using, 89, 107, 110, 113, 117, 126, 152
Stoneflies: adult forms of, 21; described, 57, 60–64; early orange, 64; emergence of, 57, 58 (fig.); golden, 63, 89, 105; imitations of, 57, 59 (fig.), 60–64; life stages of, 57, 60–64; little brown, 2, 63, 64, 103, 120; little green, 63, 92, 105; little red, 64; notes on, 63–64; using, 101, 115, 136; winter, 64
Stonefly nymphs, described, 57, 60
Strontia Springs, fishing at, 140–41
Strontia Springs Dam, 139
Stuck-in-Shucks, 54; described, 56; using, 103, 115, 117, 122
Subsurface adult caddis, described, 28–31